DATE DUE

MAR 2 2 '77			
SEP 1 '77			
FEB 2 1 '78			
MAY 2 1978			

Needlepoint from America's Great Quilt Designs

Needlepoint from America's Great Quilt Designs

Written and stitched by
Mary Kay Davis and Helen Giammattei

Illustrated by Elizabeth Meyer

Photographed by Mason Pawlak of
Boulevard Photographic, Inc.

WP

WORKMAN PUBLISHING COMPANY, NEW YORK

Workman Publishing Company
231 East 51st Street
New York, New York 10022

Book design by Paul Hanson
Illustrations by Elizabeth Meyer
Photographs by Mason Pawlak
Color work by Scala Fine Arts
Typeset by Innovative Graphics Int'l.
Printed and bound by the George Banta Company

ISBN:
Hardbound—0-911104-42-9
Paperback—0-911104-41-0

First printing, October 1974

3 4 5 6 7 8 9 10

TO MIKE AND FRANK,

our husbands
Their support, their talent, and their time
made this book possible.

Acknowledgements

When we began this book, we realized that its success would depend upon the talent and goodwill of many other people. To good friends and museum personnel who helped, our very sincere thanks.

We are particularly grateful to Al Lee and Jack Kausch, who helped us at the beginning; to our students Betsy Taylor, Emily Strain and Barbara Pierce; and to Robert Bishop and Dorothy Peers of the Henry Ford Museum.

The kindness of the following members of museum staffs is very much appreciated: Elva Adams of the Warren County Historical Society, Louise Belden of Winterthur, Linda Baumgarten of the Valentine Museum, Marilynn Bordes of the American Wing of the Metropolitan, Kathy Dirks of the Smithsonian, and Lea Rosson of the University of Kansas Museum of Art. They gave generously of their time and expertise and we are grateful.

Thanks also go to Ann Whitley and Barbara Makinson who loaned us quilts, to Dick Crandall of Boulevard Photographic, Inc., and to Mary Ann Schwartz and Marylyn Doyle.

Finally, thanks and love to our patient children, especially to our stitchers—Betsy Davis and Jane Giammattei—and to Penny, John, Bruce and Pres who helped on the home front.

Preface

Needlepoint is fun. It's creative, challenging and personal. Needlepoint designs should be exciting, innovative and glorious.

We teach a creative form of needlepoint known as canvas embroidery using antique embroidery stitches on canvas, and we are always looking for new and intriguing designs. It occurred to us that the great quilt patterns, with their colors and traditional motifs, would be beautiful worked on canvas. We asked ourselves if it were possible to combine the skills of quilting and canvas embroidery to achieve a new look in needlepoint. We tried and were enormously thrilled with capturing the subtleness of color and seductive quality of quilt patterns on canvas. In our enthusiasm we put together this book to share our collection of favorite designs.

Because we want you to enjoy working these designs as much as we did, we have made them simple to follow. We used easy and common stitches—and only a few. We show each design in full color so that you can visualize exactly what it looks like finished. Every design is shown again in a large black and white photograph with each strand of yarn easily seen. Diagrams of each design are clear, easy to read and indicate color changes in the pattern. Additionally, the section of canvas which is graphed is outlined by a box on the photograph for easy identification. And we have kept the stitching directions to a minimum.

Beginners will find designs for their projects. Experienced needlewomen will find patterns which challenge their competence. There is something here for everyone!

Enjoy these designs. We think you will agree it is a wonderful new approach to an old craft and a delightful way to bring heirloom art into your home.

THE HUSBAND'S COMPLAINT

I hate the name of German Wool
In all its colours bright,
Of chairs and stools in fancy work
I hate the very sight!
The rugs and slippers that I've seen,
The ottomans and bags;
Sooner than wear a stitch on me
I'd walk the street in rags.

Oh, Heaven preserve me from a wife
With "fancy work" run wild,
And hands which never do aught else
For husband or for child.
Our clothes are rent, our bills unpaid,
Our house is in disorder
And all because my lady-wife
Has taken to embroider!

From *British & American Tapestries*
by Mary Eirwen Jones

Contents

On Quilt Designs

Many thousands of patchwork quilts have been stitched since the first Europeans settled in America. Most of these were used until they fell into shreds and were discarded, but some still survive. Of these quilts, a number can be seen in museum collections or discovered in antique shops. Many more are hidden away in the trunks and attics of today's homes. They hold too many fond memories to be thrown away, even though they are the "wrong" color for the bedroom, or won't fit today's beds.

The designs of the old quilts intrigue us today. At first, patterns came to America from the quilter's homeland. Embroideries, samplers, designs on her treasured china, and her memories of home were reflected in a woman's quilts. But soon these motifs changed to mirror the new world around her. The Lily pattern of Elizabethan England quickly became the Virginia Lily, then the Mountain Lily of Kentucky, the Day Lily of the Midwest and finally, the Mariposa Lily of California. A woman with a memory full of English quilting patterns traveled west with a woman familiar with the Pennsylvania Dutch tradition, and they exchanged ideas along the way. They saw land and foliage change, were influenced by that change and by each other, and began stitching their old patterns in new ways.

The names given to these designs are fascinating. Sometimes they accurately pictured the life around the quilter, such as Dove in the Window, Ocean Waves, Baby Blocks and Maple Leaf. At other times, the patterns were abstract and the names reflected what was on the mind of the quilter—Burgoyne Surrounded, Garden Maze and Broken Dishes. When lives were hard, a woman's religion was all she had to fall back on and Biblical names were often attached to quilt patterns. Forbidden Fruit Tree and Star of Bethlehem are two examples.

There are two types of patchwork quilts—pieced and appliquéd. Pieced quilts are made by sewing together many small bits and pieces of cloth to form a larger piece or "top." The designs in this book are of the pieced type, since they translate well into canvas embroidery.

The importance of quilts becomes clearer when the difficulty of obtaining blankets in Colonial America is understood. Where blankets existed, they were usually homewoven of wool spun from the family's sheep. Manufactured blankets were little known in America before the nineteenth century and then were an imported luxury and very highly taxed. It was not until about the 1870s that American industry produced blankets cheaply enough to satisfy the needs of the population.

Quilts made from whole cloth, and a knowledge of quilting, came to America with the first colonists. When the Pilgrims arrived at Plymouth, the winters were bitter and the environment much rougher than they had anticipated. Their quilts began wearing out and no new cloth could be obtained, so they patched the available bedding any way they could. Such crisis periods occurred many times as America was settled. When additional coverings had to be made, scraps of precious fabric were stitched together in jigsaw-puzzle fashion. This patched fabric would be made into a bag. Dried grass, leaves, and moss were among the quilt stuffings early settlers were forced to use to survive the winters of a new settlement. This was the first period of American quilting.

As life became a bit easier, the changes appeared in the patterns of the quilts. Tops made from sheets of new cloth, in the old European tradition, were still too expensive for the colonists to afford. New cloth was costly, but patches cut from used clothing and household textiles could be pieced together in simple or elaborate geometric patterns. The hard pioneer life offered women few artistic outlets. They could garden, if enough land were cleared; they might weave or embroider if they had the looms or yarns, and they could quilt. Of those early women, many were uprooted and jolted across a continent in wagons, many more watched their loved ones die from sickness or accident, and most were poor. Yet within the limitations and hardships that life imposed upon them, these women succeeded in creating the glory of their quilts. Most of the designs in this book stem from this period—the second—of quilting.

For the few wealthy settlers, either in Northern cities or on Southern plantations, elaborate quilts were part of the interior decoration of the room, often having design elements that matched draperies or dust ruffles. Appearance was more important than economy in this third period of American quilting and

appliquéd quilts made from new cloth were not uncommon in affluent homes.

These three periods of American quilts occurred over and over as the frontier moved west. When the wilderness was opened, the first requirement was warmth, later came order, and finally, in some instances, came luxury. Intricacy of design, colors used, and free time for sewing indicated how well life was going.

Sewing lessons began very early in a girl's life for they were an essential part of her education. Women sewed all the clothing and bedding for their families, and as soon as a child could handle her needle, she began to learn its use. One of her early projects would have been the first of the thirteen quilts which tradition dictated should be in her bridal chest when she married. The first quilt top was very simple, but they became more difficult as the girl gained experience. She had twelve quilts to finish. The thirteenth, or Bride's Quilt, would not be started before her engagement. This most elaborate of the quilts was cherished and used for "best," and is the most likely to have lasted until today. An invitation to quilt the Bride's Quilt was the equivalent of today's engagement party.

Quilting satisfied various needs for the women who were our ancestors. It provided necessary warmth for their families, and at the same time, gave the women themselves artistic and social outlets. The fact that this craft and its magnificent patterns still have a place in our lives after three hundred years attests to its vitality.

A Dozen Helpful Hints

1. Gauge is the size of the canvas mesh. A #14 canvas has 14 threads per inch and is finer than #10 canvas with 10 threads to the inch.

2. Fewer strands of yarn are needed on finer gauge canvas than on larger gauge canvas. Consult the Canvas-Needle-Yarn Chart (page 165) to determine how many strands of a particular yarn you should use for your size canvas. For instance, we recommend 2 single strands of Persian yarn for #14 canvas.

3. A Straight Stitch is one that lies parallel with the threads of the canvas, either horizontally or vertically.

4. A Diagonal Stitch is one that lies diagonally covering crossed threads of the canvas.

5. Count the threads of canvas, not the canvas holes. Many stitches may use the same hole; each stitch covers a specific number of threads.

6. When a straight stitch meets a diagonal stitch, one must overlap the other so that the canvas does not show. This is diagrammed in the patterns and mentioned in the stitching directions. Always allow the pattern to overlap the background. When using diagonal tent for background, tuck the final tent stitch under the first straight stitch of the pattern.

7. Flatten the yarn. When stitching with more than one strand of yarn in the needle, keep the strands side-by-side like railroad tracks instead of twisted like a candy cane. The yarn will cover the canvas better and will produce a more uniform surface.

8. When light and dark yarn share holes, stray fibers of the dark yarn may be picked up by the light-colored yarn. To prevent this, work the areas using light-colored yarn first, if possible. If not, avoid splitting the dark yarn with the light yarn. Stitch using two motions —needle up in an empty hole and down in the hole containing the dark yarn.

9. Keep as much yarn on the back of the canvas as on the front to improve wear and appearance. Do not try to economize. Keep the tension of the yarn as even as possible. Let it lie upon the surface of the canvas—not loosely, but not pulled too tight. This is especially true with diagnoal stitches, for many overly tight diagonal stitches will warp the canvas out of shape.

10. Start stitching in the center of the canvas with the center of the design unless specifically directed to do otherwise.

11. Be gentle with the canvas. If you cannot reach the center of your work easily, roll the excess canvas; do not crease, wrinkle or crumple it. Leave a minimum of 1½" unworked canvas on all four sides. This is necessary for blocking and finishing.

12. All the designs photographed in this book list the dimensions of the work and the size of canvas used. To change the size of the design: enlarge (or reduce) each segment of the pattern by making each stitch longer (or shorter) and increase (or decrease) the number of stitches per segment. Increase (or decrease) the gauge of the canvas. Consult the Canvas Conversion Chart (page 166) for specifics. The Tree of Life and Virginia Lily variations have been enlarged by this method.

1. English Ivy Leaf, p. 126
2. Little Beech Tree, p. 124
3. Basket, p. 116
4. Fish Block, p. 58

5. Ohio Peony, p. 109
6. Feathered Star, p. 28
7. Little Red Schoolhouse, p. 60
8. Autumn Leaf, p. 132

9. Maple Leaf, p. 128
10. Twinkling Star, p. 40
11. Kansas Sunflower, p. 109
12. Sweet Gum Leaf, p. 130

1

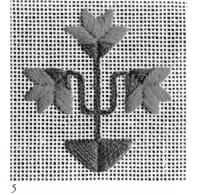

5

9

2

6

10

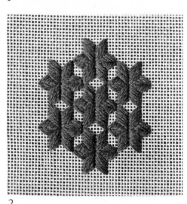

3

7

11

4

8

1. Gobelin Borders, p. 142

2. Ribbon Borders, p. 152

3. Star Borders, p. 148

4. Wild Geese Borders, p. 156

1

3

2

4

Stars and Stripes

Star of LeMoyne

(See p. 72)   Newark Museum   Shelburne Museum

The many eight-pointed star patterns that we find in quilts are all descended from this first simple star, devised in early Louisiana and named for Jean Baptiste LeMoyne, who founded New Orleans in 1718. The quilt pattern traveled up the Mississippi and became a favorite pattern in nineteenth century New England after the Louisiana Purchase of 1803. "LeMoyne" was too "Frenchified" for the New England ladies of that day and the pattern was rechristened the Lemon Star, which is still its name in the Northeast.

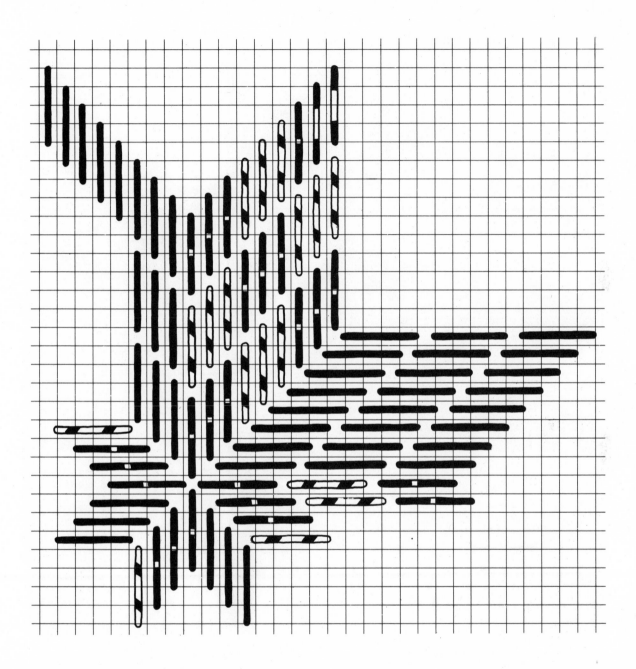

Stitching Directions. Begin in the center of the canvas and stitch one of the checkered diamonds in colors #1 and #2. Work the star's remaining three checkered diamonds. Stitch solid diamonds in color #3, noting that there are 8 instead of 9 stitches in each row. The recommended background stitch is diagonal tent. The finished pattern measures 3½″ square when worked on #14 canvas.

Broken Star—LeMoyne

(See p. 72)

When stars became popular quilt patterns in the nineteenth century, it was soon discovered that the star's diamond shaped segments could be broken apart and regrouped into a larger, more sophisticated composition. The design was named the broken star, and its appearance could vary greatly depending upon the pattern of the parent star.

Stitching Directions. Begin in the center of the canvas and stitch one of the checkered diamonds in colors #1 and #2. Work the star's remaining three checkered diamonds. Stitch the solid diamonds in color #3, noting that there are 8 instead of 9 stitches in each row. Work the outer ring, so that dark points touch dark diamonds and checkered points touch checkered diamonds. Note that diamonds in outer halo have varying stitch counts. The recommended background stitch is diagonal tent. The finished star measures 7″ square when worked on #14 canvas.

Blue Star

(See p. 19)

Eight-pointed stars are familiar to quiltmakers. The eight diamonds that form the star were not difficult for an experienced needlewoman to cut and sew, and the finished pattern lent itself to many different compositions. In needlepoint, there are many ways to stitch a star. The Blue Star utilizes subtle color shadings to achieve its crystalline effect.

Stitching Directions. Start in center of star with color #1, the darkest shade. Work the next rings in shades #2, #3, and #4. Begin decreasing for points on the following ring, using shade #3, then #2. Work the points in shade #1. The recommended background stitch is diagonal tent. The finished pattern measures 3½″ square when worked on #14 canvas.

Feathered Star

(See p.18)   Newark Museum   Smithsonian Institution

The Feathered Star has also been called the Sawtooth Star. The oldest example known to us was made in 1771 as a gift to a twelve-year-old girl, ancestor of the present owner. The design was a favorite in antebellum Virginia.

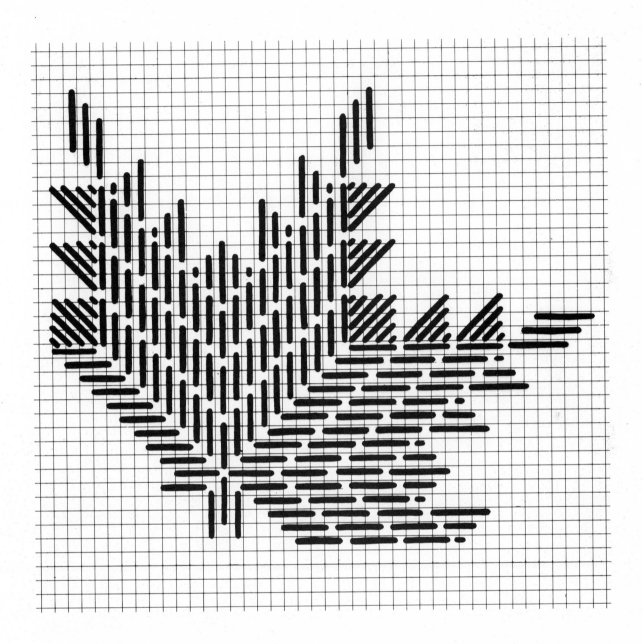

Stitching Directions. Start at the center of the star and work three "V" rows to form one side. Repeat on the other three sides completing the star. Add "feathers" around the edge. The recommended background stitch is diagonal tent. The finished pattern measures 4¼" when worked on #14 canvas.

Star of Bethlehem

(See p. 75)   Newark Museum   Valentine Museum

The Star of Bethlehem is the most familiar of the many eight-pointed star patterns. Star quilts were made of small diamonds pieced together and were a test of a needlewoman's skill. Because such quilts were treasured for "best," many have lasted into the twentieth century.

Star of the East and Eight-Pointed Star were other names for this majestic pattern.

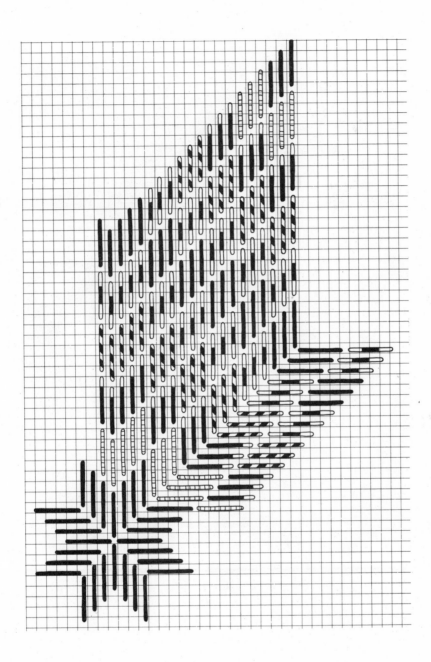

Stitching Directions. Stitch the center of the star in the middle of the canvas, using color #1. Work the next ring in color #2. Work the next four rings in colors #3, #4, #5 and #6. Begin decreasing for star points on the next ring, using color #5. Continue decreasing with colors #4, #3, #2. Finally work the star points in color #1. The recommended background stitch is diagonal tent. The border is Star of LeMoyne (see p. 151). The finished pattern measures 10½" square when worked on #14 canvas.

Broken Star—Bethlehem

(See p. 74) Henry Ford Museum

In this variation on the traditional Star of Bethlehem the diamond shaped segments, from which the central eight-pointed star is made, are separated and regrouped to form the radiating halo. In different times and places, it has also been called Carpenter's Wheel, Double Star, Star within a Star and Dutch Rose.

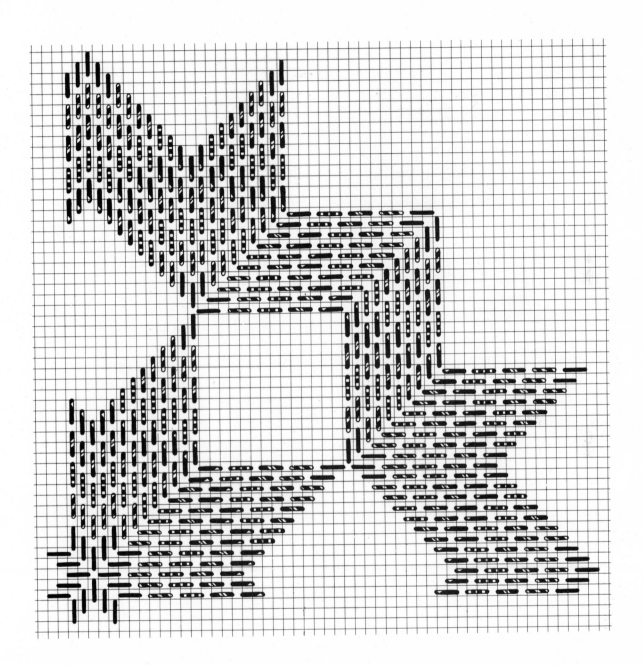

Stitching Directions. To make the diagram easier to follow, color each of the symbols with a colored pencil or pen before stitching.

Begin in the center and work the central star in color #1. Change to color #2 and work the ring around the star.

Continue, following the diagram, until the pattern is complete. The recommended background stitch is diagonal tent. The finished pattern measures 7″ when worked on #14 canvas.

Falling Star

(See p. 70)

This decorative version of the basic Star of LeMoyne gives a feeling of motion within the star's outline. Possibly for that reason, it also was known as Flying Star, Circling Swallows, and Flying Swallow. The pattern dates from about 1800 and was a great favorite in New England and Pennsylvania.

The pattern shows off the gloss of the wool beautifully, but because of the length of the individual stitches, it will not wear well. Use the Falling Star where you can enjoy its beauty and not snag its yarn.

Stitching Directions. Start at the center, working all eight triangles in color #1. Let the diagonal stitches overlap the straight stitches. Stitch the eight three-pointed stars in color #2, noting the blunted innermost point on alternate stars. Tuck the stitches by the blunt points under the central triangles. Complete the star with color #3, again allowing the diagonal stitches to overlap the straight stitches. Note that the triangle bases overlap also. The finished pattern measures 6" square when worked on #14 canvas.

Seven Sisters and Variation

(See p. 19)

Atlas, the Titan who held up the heavens in Greek mythology, had seven daughters who were turned into stars by the gods. These stars, called the Seven Sisters, form a constellation known as the Pleiades and were a familiar sight to our ancestors.

A quilt of six-pointed stars could only be pieced by an excellent nee-

dlewoman. Eight-pointed stars could be cut fairly easily by folding the cloth in half, in fourths and into eighths before cutting. A six-pointed star, however, depended upon folding material into equal thirds and then into sixths. Therefore, six-pointed star quilts were difficult to make and rare.

A snowflake pattern forms around the

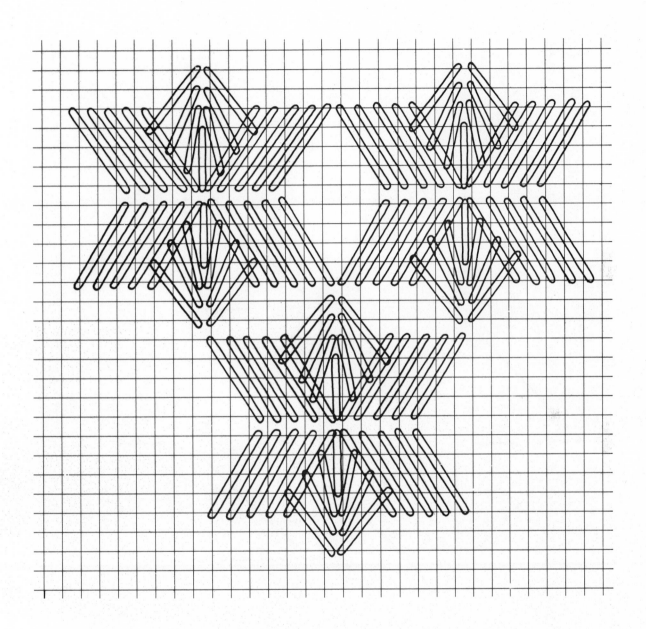

center of the star cluster when it is worked in one color. If the stars are stitched in two colors, as in the variation, the design changes dramatically.

Stitching Directions. Begin the central star by stitching the top and bottom points. Next work the remaining four star points, allowing the diagonal stitches to overlap top and bottom. Stitch the remaining six stars in the cluster. Where star points meet, they share the same hole in the canvas. The recommended background stitch is diagonal tent. The finished pattern measures 3¼" x 2¾" when worked on #14 canvas.

Seven Sisters Variation

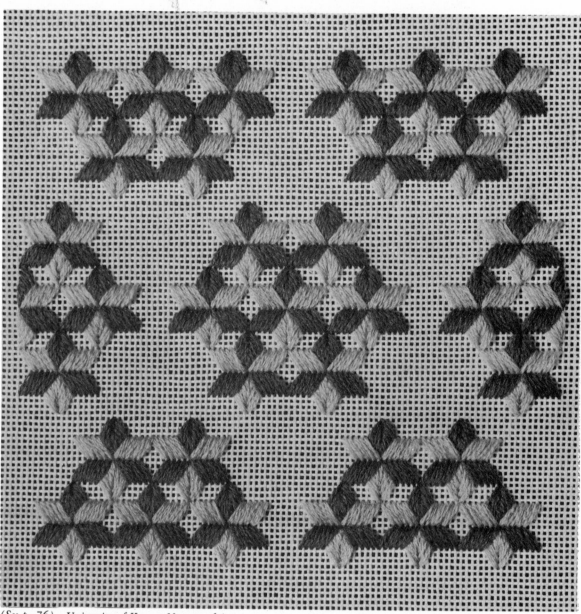

(See p. 76)   University of Kansas Museum of Art

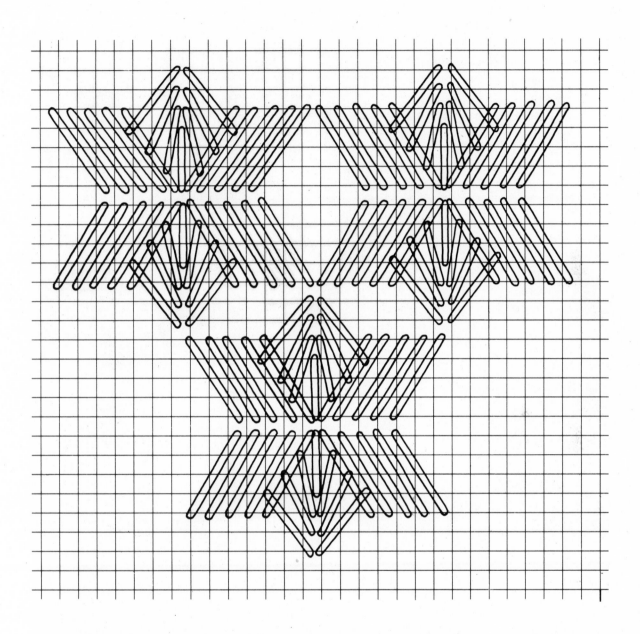

Stitching Directions for Seven Sisters Variation. Work central star by stitching top point in color #1 and, next, the bottom point in color #2. Work the bottom two side-points in color #1, allowing the diagonal stitches to overlap the bottom point. Stitch the top two side-points in color #2, letting stitches overlap. Stitch the remaining stars in the cluster to match the central one. The recommended background is diagonal tent. The finished pattern measures 7″ x 6½″ when worked on #14 canvas.

Twinkling Star

(See p.18)

Other names for this design were Star Puzzle and Pieced Star, which give a clue to its origin. A pieced star could be made from bits of cloth—"pieced" or "puzzled" together. It was more economical than a star of the same size made from whole cloth. Creative solutions to the problem of lack of cloth produced some of the most beautiful patterns that come down to us today. Note the Windmill, a design in its own right, in the star's center.

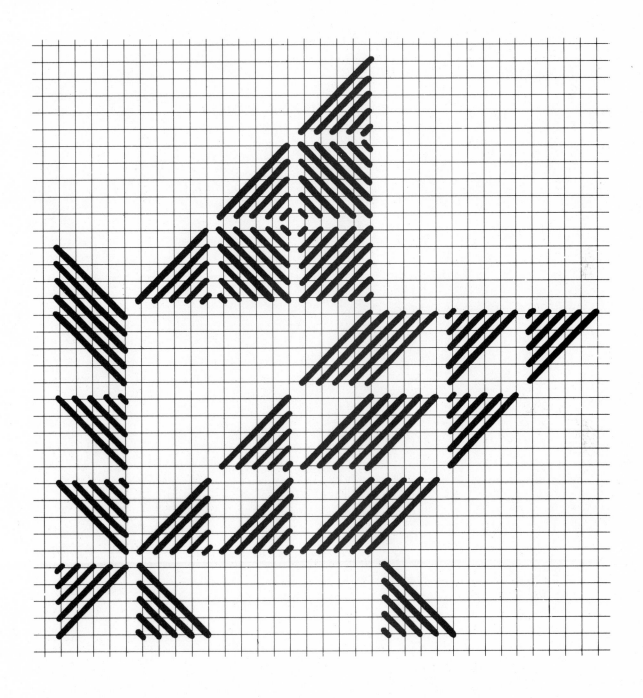

Stitching Directions. Start at the star's center and work small pinwheel with color #1. Continue to stitch as diagrammed with color #1. Fill in un-worked area with color #2. The finished pattern measures 4½″ square when worked on #14 canvas.

Stars and Stripes

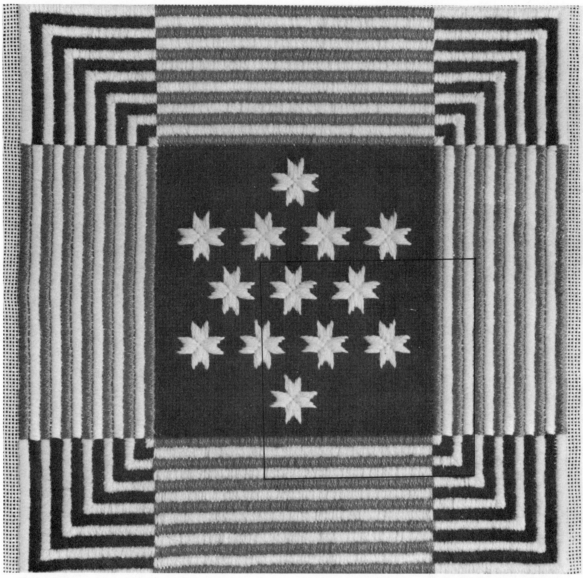

(See p. 72)

Americans have been intensely proud of their country since its birth, and this pride has taken concrete form in the decorative arts. After 1776, stars, eagles and shields abounded on pottery, textiles, furniture and quilts.

Patriotic quilts tended to be one-of-a-kind designs that reflected the patriotism of the individual who pieced them. This pattern originated in Hawaii in the 1890s. It was a time of unrest in the Islands when pro- and anti-American sentiments ran high. Queen Liliuokalani, the last of the Hawaiian monarchs, was deposed in 1893 and the new provisional government immediately applied for American annexation, which was granted in 1898.

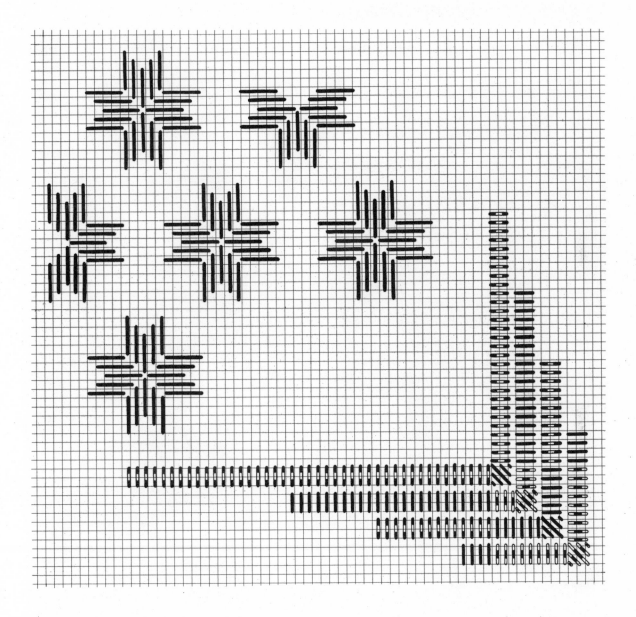

Stitching Directions. Stitch the central star in middle of canvas. Work remaining stars, counting carefully to position them correctly. Work red and white stripes alternately—do not work red stripes first and then try to fill in with white. The white yarn will pick up red fibers. Work blue and white corners in the same manner. Fill in the center using diagonal tent stitch. The finished pattern measures 11 ¾" square when worked on #14 canvas.

Red, White and Blue Star

(See p. 19)

When the Star of LeMoyne (see p. 22) was sewed from striped fabrics, the resulting pattern often gave the effect of a pinwheel. When the stripes were red, white and blue, the pinwheel was also patriotic. This quilt was stitched in 1855 when the approaching Civil War made many Americans fear for the Republic.

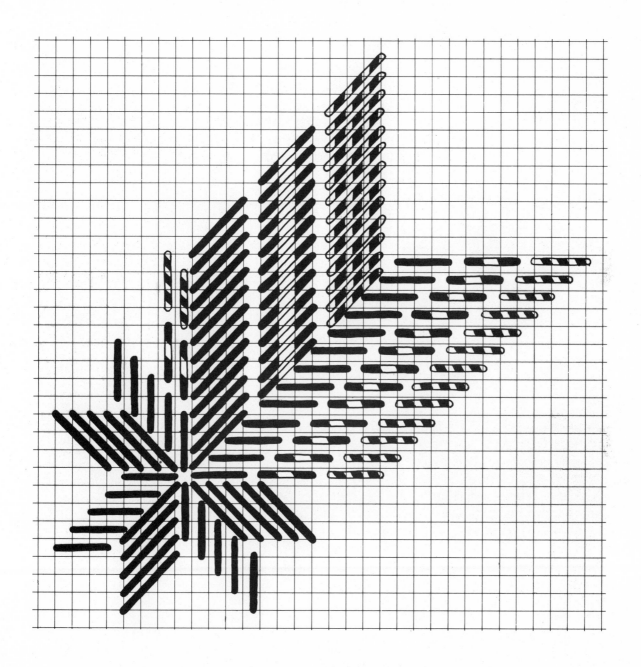

Stitching Directions. Work one star point at a time. Start at the center of the canvas with red yarn and work all 13 stitches. Repeat with white and then blue. Work each succeeding point of the star in the same sequence by color. The finished pattern measures 3½″ square when worked on #14 canvas.

Burgoyne Surrounded

(See p. 70) University of Kansas Museum of Art   Henry Ford Museum

In 1777 the British general John Burgoyne tried to take the city of Albany, New York, but was surrounded by the Americans and surrendered at Saratoga on October 17th. This early victory gave the Revolutionary forces the strength to fight on and helped convince the French to become our allies.

Burgoyne Surrounded was also called Burgoyne's Surrender and is a quilt pattern from the early nineteenth century. Later, the name changed and the quilt was known as the Wheel of Fortune until approximately 1850. By 1860, from Ohio westward, it was called The Road to California.

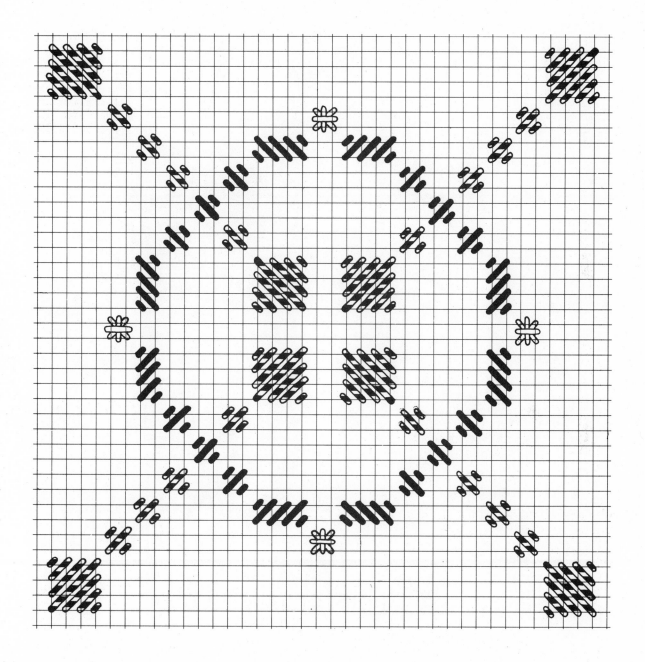

Stitching Directions. Start in the center of the canvas with color #1 and work the four central squares. Work each diagonal arm to the next set of large squares. Be sure to leave space on each arm for the octagon in color #2. We recommend diagonal tent stitch for the background. The finished pattern measures 6″ square when worked on #14 canvas.

Yankee Pride

(See p. 70) *Valentine Museum   University of Kansas Museum of Art*

The American colonists' pride in their new country and its destiny enabled them to withstand dangers and setbacks with the faith that the future would be better. All early Americans were "Yankees," to differentiate them from the British, until the Civil War gave the word a specifically Northern meaning.

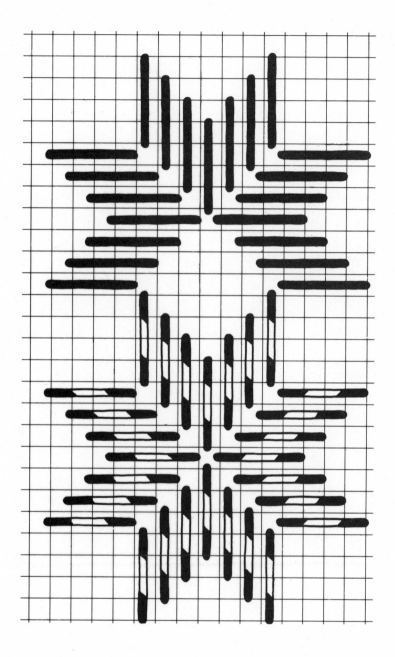

Stitching Directions. Work the central star of the top section in color #1. Stitch the surrounding six-pointed stars in color #2, making sure that the tips of the stars share the same hole. Work the remaining sections. This design can be worked as an overall pattern although it was not used that way historically. The recommended background stitch is diagonal tent. The finished pattern measures 6¼″ square when worked on #14 canvas.

Nautical and Nostalgia

Ocean Waves

(See p. 71)   Smithsonian Institution

The Ocean Waves is one of our country's great nautical quilt patterns. These quilts were designed along the North Atlantic coast from Maine to Long Island. Wives and daughters of seamen—fishermen, whalers and China traders—spent much of their lives looking out to sea waiting for their men to come home. Such old patterns as the Ship's Wheel from Cape Cod, the Fish Block, Clam Shell, and the Ocean Waves reflect the sea as a vital force in the lives of the quilters.

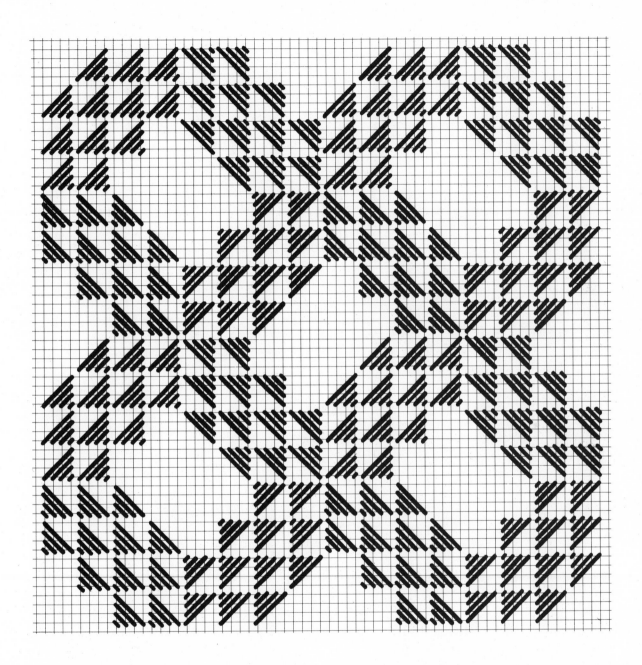

Stitching Directions. Start at center of canvas with small pinwheel in color #1. Each large blade of pinwheel consists of 12 triangles. Stitch one blade—its farthest tip will be one segment of the next small pinwheel. Finish the background by filling in each small triangle with color #2 to form small squares. Fill open areas with the same small squares, using only color #2. The finished pattern measures 6″ x 5″ when worked on #14 canvas.

Ship's Wheel

(See p. 75)   Arizona Historical Society   Valentine Museum

In the early days when all settlements hugged the Atlantic coast, this pattern was a favorite in New England. The tips of the design represented the wheel's handles. As the years went by, women from Cape Cod and northern New England moved westward, taking the pattern with them. Their daughters grew up inland, never having seen a ship, and they redesigned and renamed the old Ship's Wheel. It became the Harvest Sun or Prairie Star. The empty ring between the wheel's center and its rim was filled with a third color, making a radiating sun from a Yankee Clipper's wheel.

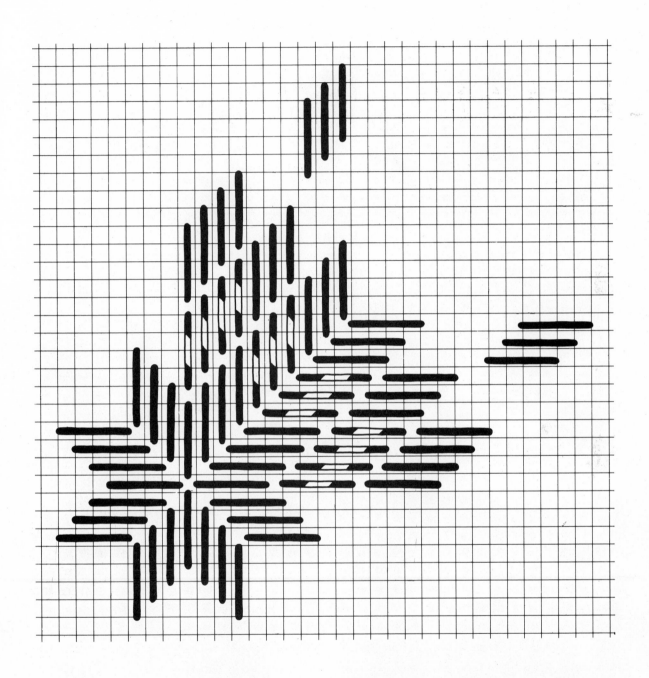

Stitching Directions. In each wheel, work the central star first, using color #1. Work the next ring in color #2. The third ring is worked in color #1. Stitch the tips in color #1. Work the background in diagonal tent stitch and color #2. The finished pattern measures 7¼″ square when worked on #14 canvas.

Clam Shell

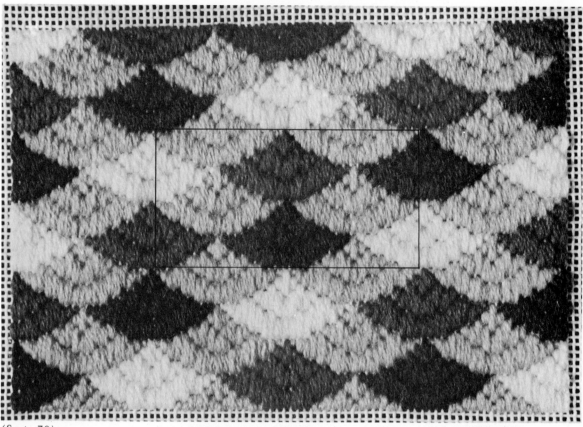

(See p. 70)

This design was a popular nautical pattern along the North Atlantic seaboard, and the majority of Clam Shell quilts were pieced in New England during the eighteenth century. This pattern may have been inspired by the stylized ocean waves embroidered on Chinese silks that were often among the gifts brought home to New England by the China traders.

The curved outlines of the Clam Shell make it a tricky pattern to piece successfully. It may have been partially because of its difficulty that the design went out of fashion as a pieced pattern in the early 1800s. However, as a pattern for quilting, it is a classic still in use today. When the circles were small, they were often traced around the quilter's thimble, and the finely quilted result was known as "thimble quilting."

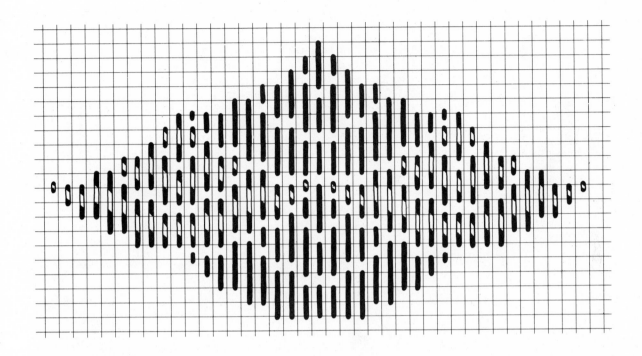

Stitching Directions. Begin at the point of any clam shell. Work the three rings. Stitch the adjoining shell, making sure that two threads of canvas separate one shell's tip from another. This is for the bottom stitch of the shell on the row above. Finish each row of shells before beginning the next row. Shell colors can be varied, but use more than one color or the individual motifs will disappear. The finished pattern measures 6″ x 4″ when worked on #14 canvas.

Fish Block

(See p.18)

The Fish Block, or Gold Fish, is a nautical version of the basic eight-pointed star. It is a fresh and realistic design with a light-hearted touch.

In colonial times, fish were a vital source of food and income up and down the Atlantic coast. Theologically, they have been a Christian symbol since the earliest days of the Church.

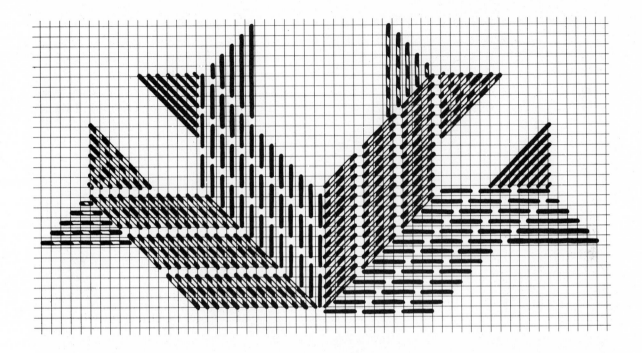

Stitching Directions. Start one fish at the center of the canvas and complete, using color #1. Work the adjoining fish in color #2. Complete the star, alternating colors. Note the overlap of diagonal and straight stitches. Stitch eyes with French knots in color #3. The recommended background stitch is diagonal tent. The finished pattern measures 6″ square when worked on #10 canvas.

Little Red Schoolhouse

(See p.18)   Smithsonian Institution

This quaint pattern seems to have originated in New Jersey around the 1870s. It is reminiscent of schoolmarms and potbellied stoves, and is an example of the pictorial designs that became popular with quilters after the end of the Civil War.

The Little Red Schoolhouse lends itself to a needlepoint piece for a child's room, or as the focus for some small item such as a purse.

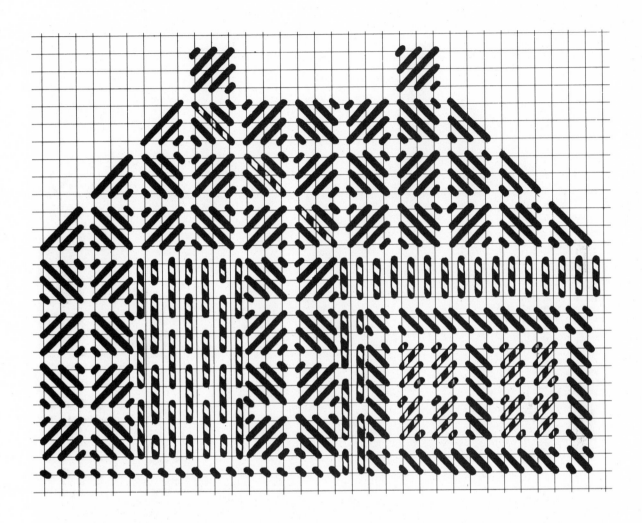

Stitching Directions. Work roof and chimneys with color #1. Work the edge of the roof in color #2. Stitch the front and side of schoolhouse in color #1. Then stitch the door, windows, eaves and corner of the house in color #2. A French knot in color #1 for a door handle is optional. The finished pattern measures 2½″ x 2″ when worked on #14 canvas.

Dove in the Window

(See p. 19)

In earlier days, pigeon pie was a familiar dish and to help provide it barns were built with windows in the gables through which the pigeons gained access to their nests in the hay loft. These windows were often made in a decorative shape—round or octagonal—and gave an attractive touch to a barn's exterior.

Doves in the window were indeed part of many a farmyard's scene, though it must have taken an imaginative farmer's wife to come up with so delightful a pattern.

The spiral effect of the stitches that form the birds' bodies gives a sense of motion to the design.

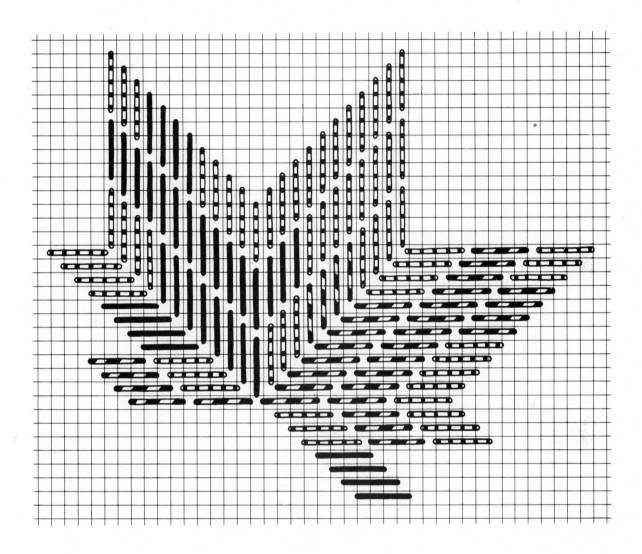

Stitching Directions. Begin in the center and stitch one dove in color #1. Work adjoining dove in color #2. Stitch the last two doves, alternating colors. Finish the star in color #3. A French knot in the center in color #4 is optional. The recommended background stitch is diagonal tent. The finished pattern measures 4″ square when worked on #14 canvas.

Cornucopia

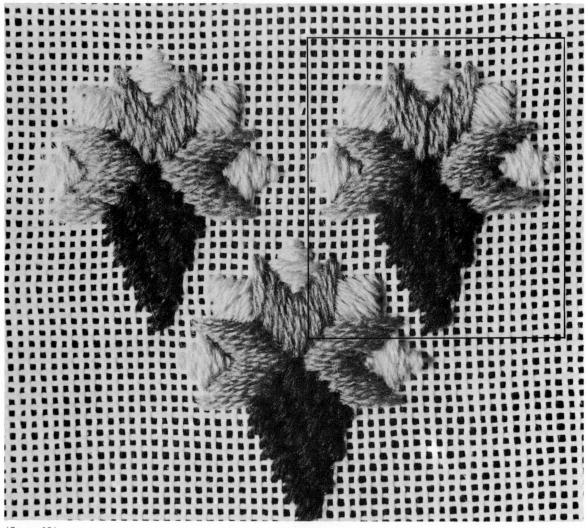

(See p. 19)

The cornucopia was a symbol of plenty in the art of Greece and Rome. During the revival of interest in classical antiquity during America's Federal period, around 1810, the cornucopia be- came a frequently used symbol of hospitality. Cornucopias were carved in wood, embroidered, and even used as elaborate centerpieces on banquet tables.

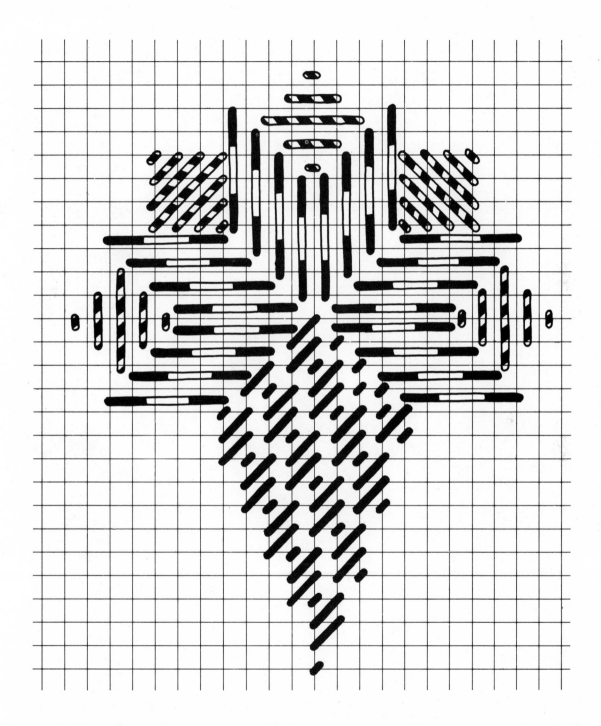

Stitching Directions. Work six-pointed star first in color #1. Add the segments around the star's rim in color #2. Work the base of cornucopia in color #3. Note overlap of diagonal and straight stitches. Cornucopias may be used as an overall pattern or, side by side, as an effective border. The recommended background stitch is diagonal tent. The finished pattern measures 3½″ square when worked on #14 canvas.

Baby Blocks

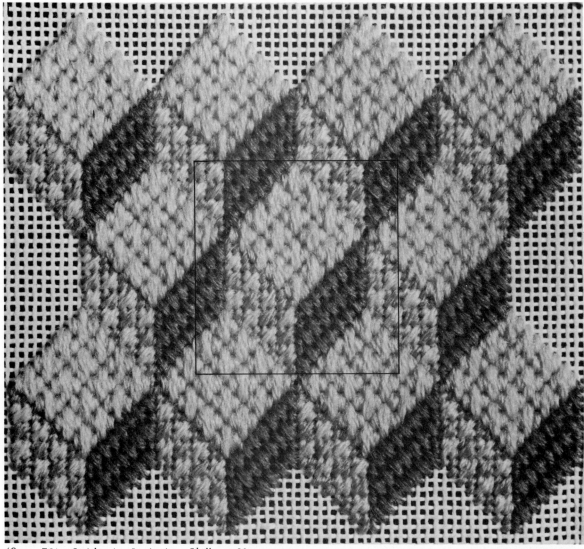

(See p. 70) Smithsonian Institution Shelburne Museum

Box Quilt and Cube Work are two other names for this design where the central blocks, arranged on their points, create an optical illusion. Place them flat on one side in another quilt pattern and a new diagonal illusion emerges. This latter pattern was known as Steps to Heaven or Pandora's Box.

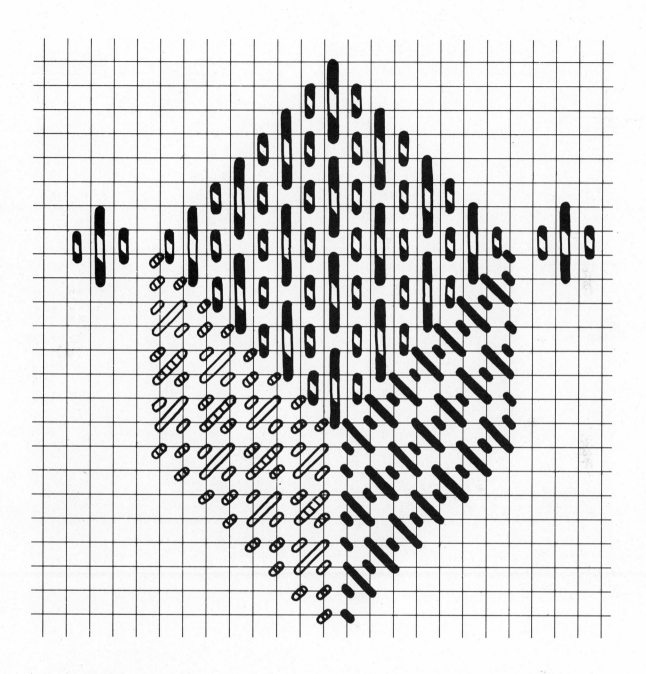

Stitching Directions. Start at center in color #1 and stitch the diamond. Work the lower left-hand side of the cube with medium colors #2 and #3. Work the lower right-hand side of the cube with your darkest color—#4. Note the overlapping of straight and diagonal stitches. The finished pattern measures 5″ x 4¼″ when worked on #14 canvas.

Sunburst Variation, p. 80

1

3

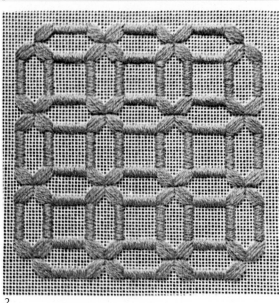

2

4

1

4

2

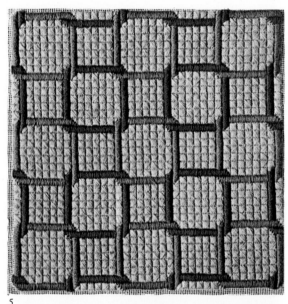

5

3

6

Broken Star—Bethlehem, p. 32

1

4

2

5

3

6

3

1

4

2

5

Overall Patterns

Sunburst and Variation

(See p. 19)

The broad, open spaces of the New World gave settlers an easy familiarity with the sky above them. Such quilt names as Moon Over the Mountain, Blazing Star, North Wind and Sunburst show the pioneer quilter's awareness of her environment.

This Sunburst pattern, or Grandma's Dream, was stitched in 1870 and is an excellent example of a "one patch" quilt. In this quilt type, the needlewoman sewed together one patch at a time, starting at the center of the quilt and working outward.

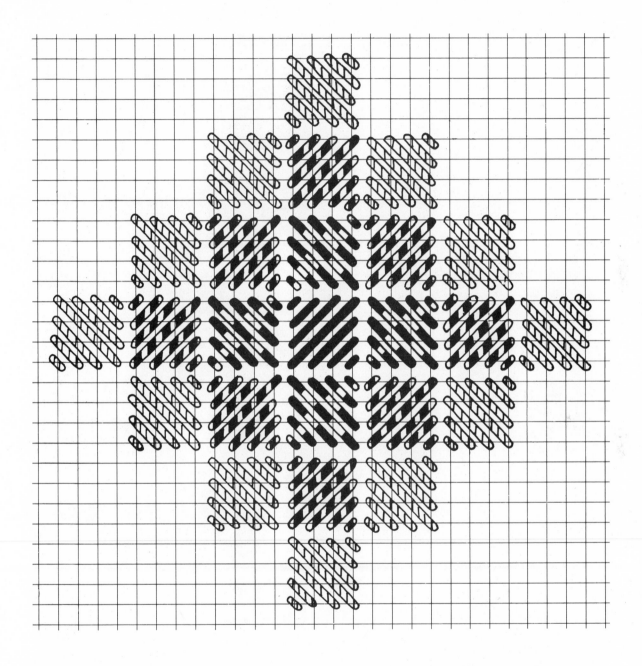

Stitching Directions. Stitch the center square in your darkest shade of color #1. Work the encircling four squares in the next lighter shade of color #1. Note that your stitches in these four squares go in opposite direction to those of the center square. Work out in increasingly larger diamonds, alternating the direction of the stitch and changing colors and shades as desired. The finished pattern measures 4″ square when worked on #14 canvas.

Sunburst Variation

(See p. 69)

Stitching Directions for Sunburst Variation. In this Sunburst variation, color changes occur at the diagonal of each little square instead of at the square's edge. This gives a smooth outline to the concentric diamonds instead of the "stair-step" edges found in the Sunburst pattern.

You can use any number of colors in this pattern, but it is most effective with two to four shades of each color. Arrange the colors in any order desired. The Amish needlewoman who designed this variation used the strong, dark colors

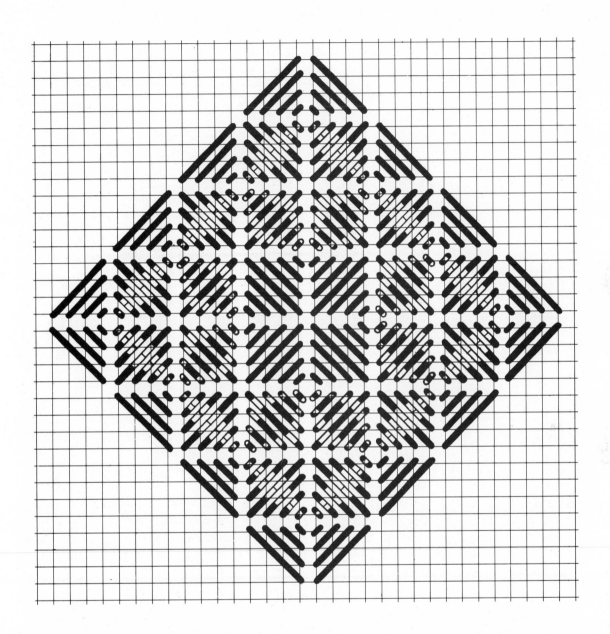

characteristic of Amish quilts.

Start in the center of the canvas and stitch the four squares in the center of the diagram. Make sure to work the second row following the direction of the stitches as diagrammed. The long stitches will form a diamond shape. Work outward in concentric diamonds with color #1 and complete the diagram. Introduce color #2 by completing squares. Continue to work in shades of color #2, #3, etc. Color changes are made when your long stitches form a smooth diamond. (See diagram) The finished pattern measures 12″ square when worked on #14 canvas.

Double Irish Chain

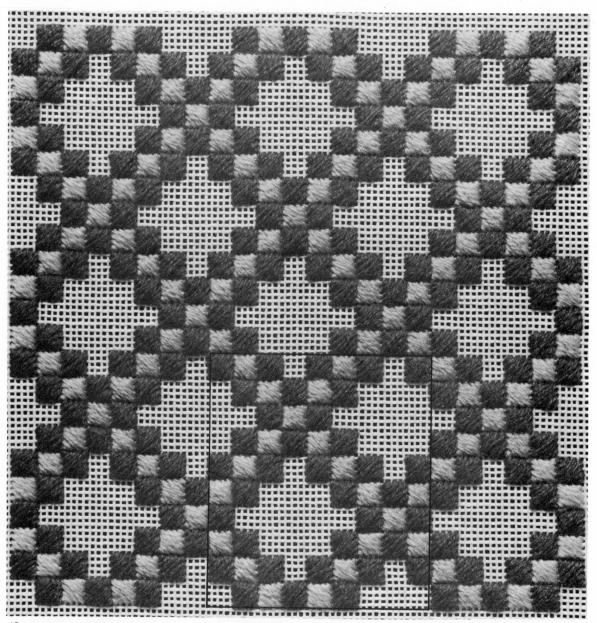

(See p. 75) *Baltimore Museum of Art   Newark Museum*

One of the oldest and most common quilt patterns is the Irish Chain. There are Single, Double and Triple Irish Chains, differing only in the number of rows of diagonally-placed blocks that crisscross the quilt's surfaces. Oddly enough, in spite of its wide distribution, this is one pattern that has never had another name, while many others seemingly have changed names every ten years or ten miles.

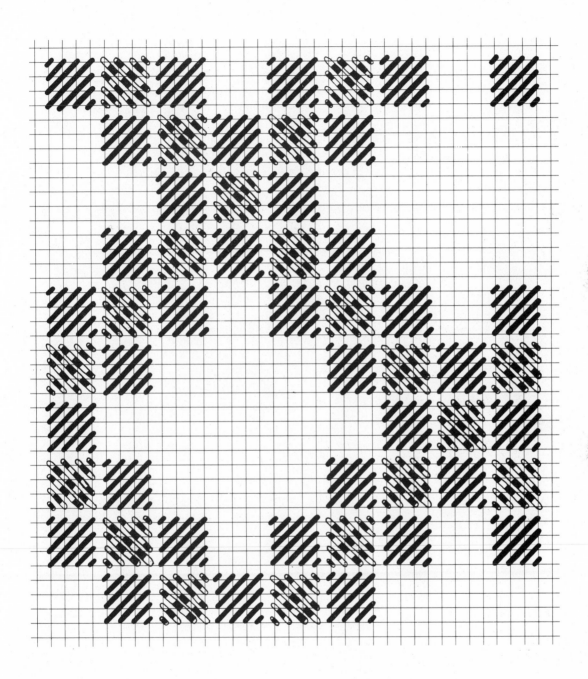

Stitching Directions. Start by out-lining the smallest diamond in the center of the canvas with 12 squares of color #1. Work the neighboring, larger diamond in color #2. Work largest diamond in color #1. Continue stitching these three rows, noting that all squares of color #1 slant in one direction, and all those of color #2, in the opposite direction. Fill centers with your chosen background color using squares like those that make up the chains, alternating direction of stitches in adjoining squares or use the diagonal tent. The finished pattern measures 7″ square when worked on #14 canvas.

Pinwheel

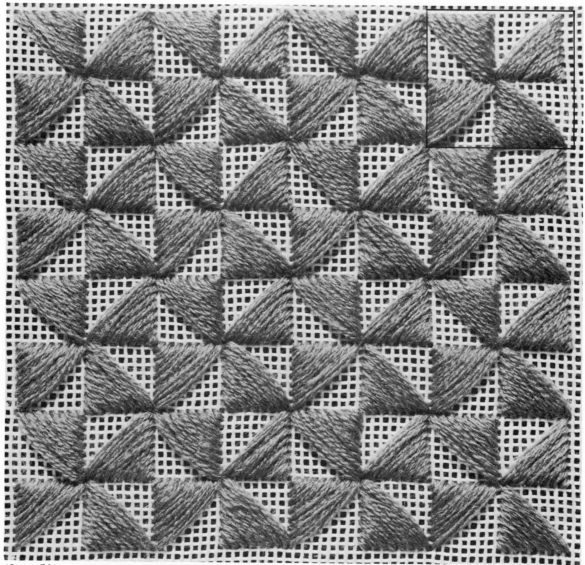

(See p. 70)   Smithsonian Institution   Shelburne Museum

Call it Pinwheel, Windmill, Water Wheel, Mill Wheel or Water Mill, this is one of the earliest pieced quilt patterns that has come down from America's past. A pinwheel pattern was easy to cut, wasted very little cloth, and produced a design with life and motion.

The individual pinwheels could be separated from each other with plain blocks, be placed diagonally like Irish Chains, or as shown here—placed side by side—where the effect was called Broken Dishes.

This is a versatile overall pattern that frequently creates optical illusions.

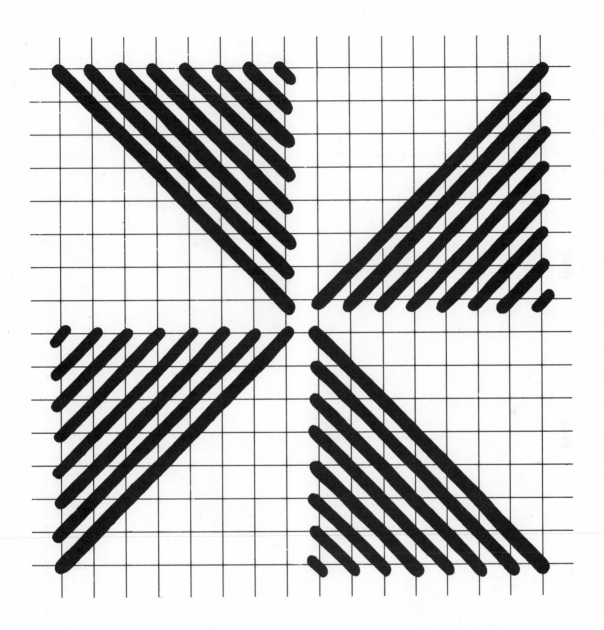

Stitching Directions. Work each pinwheel, triangle by triangle, in color #1. The longest stitches of the triangles meet and share a hole. Keep the tension of your stitches loose. Complete the background in color #2, using same stitch. Long stitches in this pattern give a bold effect, but snag easily. This makes it unsuitable for an object, such as a chair seat, that gets much wear. The finished pattern measures 6″ square when worked on #10 canvas.

Album Quilt

(See p. 72) *Baltimore Museum of Art* *Warren County Historical Society Museum*

An Album Quilt was a gift that reminded the recipient of dear friends far away. Before a minister and his wife were leaving for a new parish, when a family was moving West, or before a new bride left for her husband's home—these were occasions for an album party. The invited guests each pieced one patch and signed it. Tradition decreed that the patches had to be finished and sewed together before supper, at which point the gentlemen arrived to join the party. The top was quilted at a later date by the same friends at a party given by the guest of honor.

As a personal gift, the Album pattern serves the same function in needlepoint as it did in the quilts of years past.

Stitching Directions. Each large square of the pattern is, in turn, composed of four smaller needlepoint squares. The longest stitches of each of the four squares meet in the center. The large squares are arranged as in a checkerboard. The name is worked in tent stitch. Using a contrasting color, work the background around the name in diagonal tent stitch. Note that the diagonal stitches which form the inside and outside edges of the encircling diamond are each over eight threads of canvas.

For a coaster or pincushion of smaller size, use #12 canvas and stitch each square of the pattern over 3 threads instead of 8. Substitute initials for the name. The result is a hostess gift to be cherished.

The finished pattern measures 11″ x 11″ when worked on #10 canvas.

Delectable Mountains

(See p. 75)   Newark Museum

Two books which had a profound influence on the formation of early America were the Bible and John Bunyan's *Pilgrim's Progress*. Bunyan read the Bible and came to his own conclusions about religion, which were often in conflict with those of the established Church. *Pilgrim's Progress* was written while Bunyan was serving a term in prison for preaching his version of christianity.

In *Pilgrim's Progress*, Christian is shown the Delectable Mountains in a dream and they are " . . .beautified with woods, vineyards, fruits of all sorts, . . .and fountains, very delectable to behold." To the immigrants of England it meant the land of milk and honey which they sought. Delectable Mountains is a fitting name for a colonial quilt pattern.

The design repeats itself with expanding concentric rings.

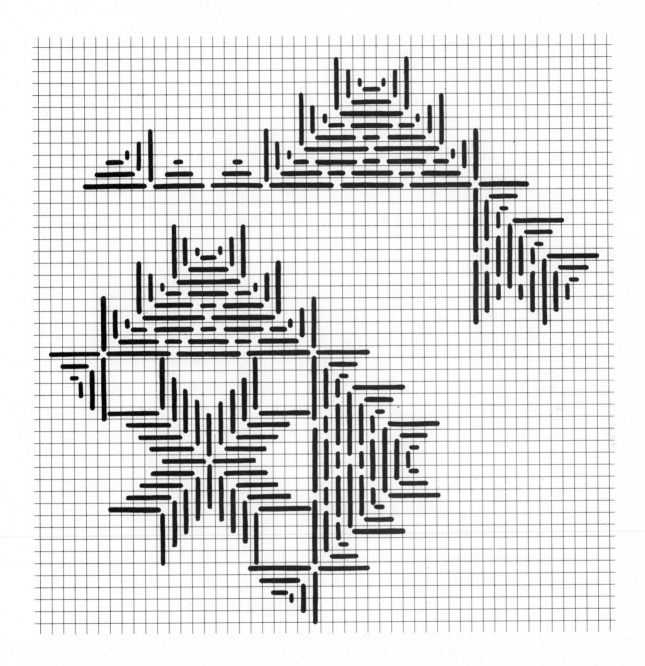

Stitching Directions. First work the central star, noting that the final stitch on each point is over 5, not 4 threads of canvas. Stitch the encircling diamond, and then the small segments around its edge. Work concentric blocks until the space is filled. The recommended background stitch is diagonal tent. The finished pattern measures 7½″ square when worked on #14 canvas.

Monkey Wrench

(See p. 71)

Monkey Wrench, Snail's Tail and Indiana Puzzle are some of the names by which this intriguing pattern was known. Though it was familiar to Indiana pioneers in the early nineteenth century, it is reminiscent of the work of such modern artists as M.C. Escher, and of the "Op" art of recent years. Whether you consider it antique or modern, the interlocking motifs produce a lively design of great visual interest.

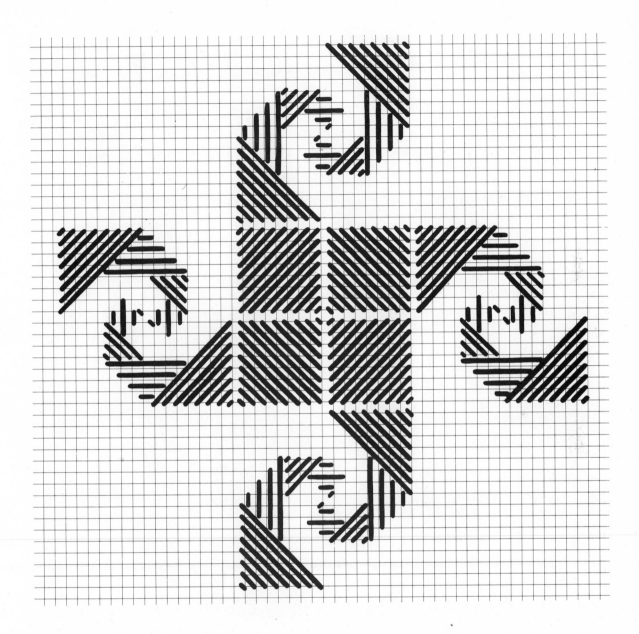

Stitching Directions. Start the center of one monkey wrench in the middle of the canvas. Stitch the central four squares as diagrammed. Then stitch four hooks, allowing the straight and diagonal stitches to overlap. Stitch the second monkey wrench, making sure that the stitches at the end of its hooks meet those of the first motif in the same hole. Fill the empty space with the same pattern stitched in another color. Work the lighter color first. The finished pattern measures 6" square when worked on #14 canvas.

Twist Patchwork

(See p. 72)

This pattern of interlocking octagons originated after the close of the Civil War, and was often worked with appliquéd ribbons. It is reminiscent of the Garden Maze, and the Double Wedding Ring quilts so popular with nineteenth century brides.

Twist Patchwork lends itself best to items of square or rectangular shape.

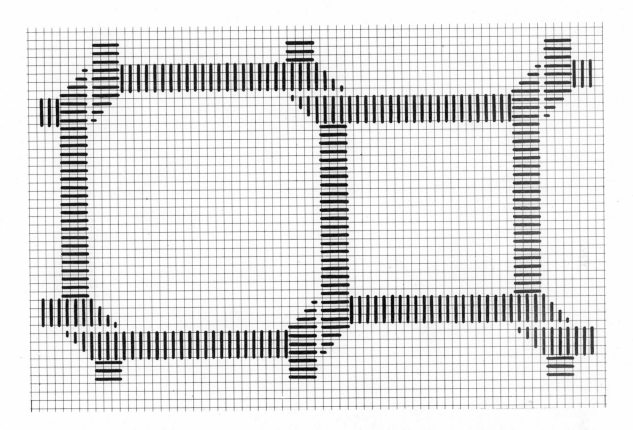

Stitching Directions. This pattern uses easy stitches, but it is necessary to count accurately. The ribbons can be all one color or alternating colors. The larger squares are 28 threads across; the smaller squares are 20 threads across. Start with a large block centered on the canvas. The finished pattern measures 11″ square when worked on #14 canvas.

Garden Maze

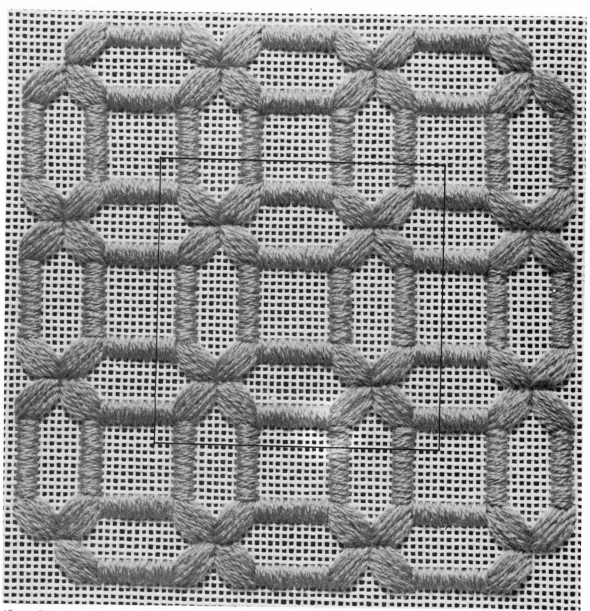

(See p. 71)   Newark Museum   Smithsonian Institution

The Garden Maze recalls the ordered world of the eighteenth century. Symmetrical, geometric plans of fine proportion formed the basis for much colonial American design. In the Georgian architecture of Sir Christopher Wren, in the formal boxwood gardens at Williamsburg, in the lattice work on a Chippendale chair—logic and order prevailed.

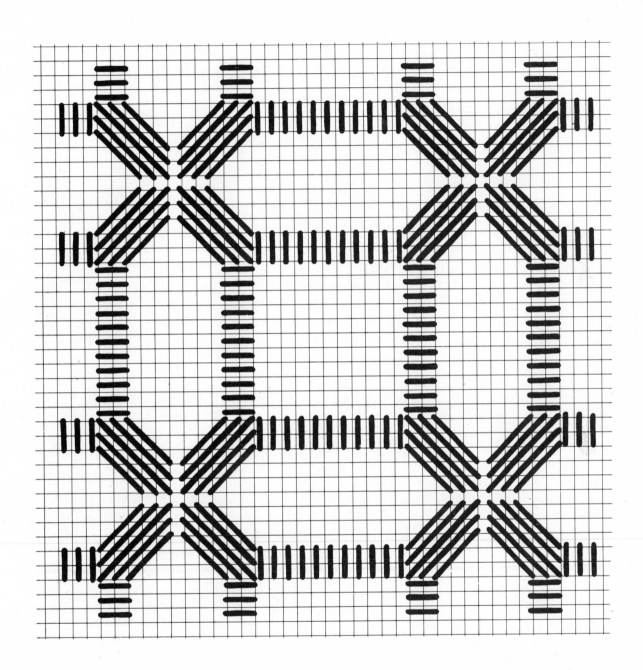

Stitching Directions. Center a small square in the middle of the canvas and outline it with straight stitches. Work diagonal "X's" at each of the square's corners. Connect the outer edge of the "X's" with straight stitches, forming the first octagon. Continue working outward. Note that the straight stitches overlap diagonal stitches.

This pattern makes an excellent belt or border. The recommended background stitch is diagonal tent. The finished pattern measures 6" square when worked on #14 canvs.

Gordian Knot

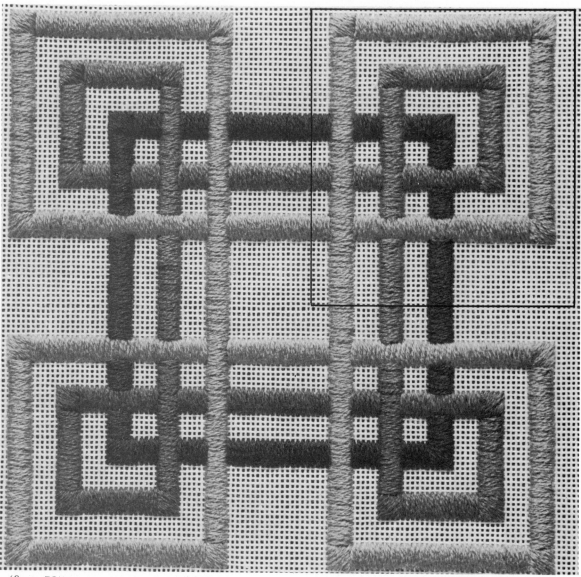

(See p. 75)

When women gained access to books and to education beyond the home, titles from Greek mythology began to appear as names for their quilts. Such a myth inspired the Gordian Knot pattern in the 1870s. According to the story, Gordius, king of Phrygia, tied a team of oxen to his chariot with a knot that, seemingly, had no beginning or end, and dedicated the oxen, cart and knot to Zeus. Unfortunately for the gift, an oracle had promised the empire of Asia to the man who could untie the knot. Alexander the Great, wishing to prove that he was destined to conquer the world, first tried to untie the knot. Then, ambitious and impatient, he slashed it in two with his sword. From that time, "To cut the Gordian Knot" has meant to solve problems using drastic measures.

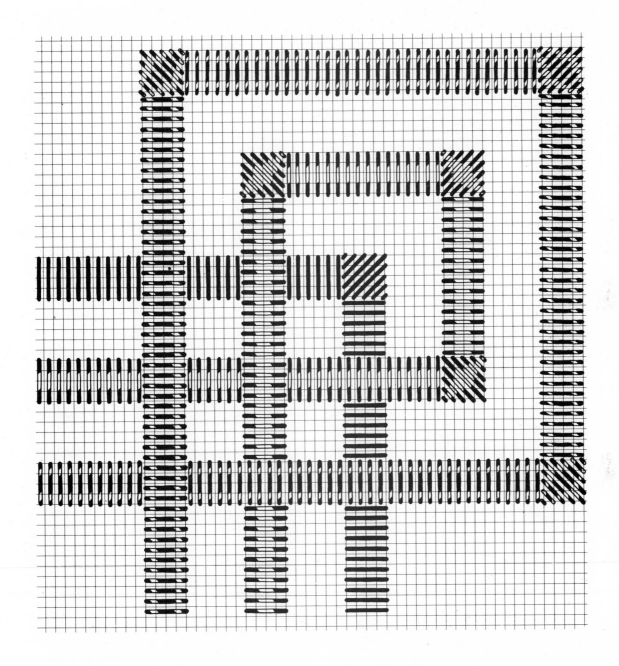

Stitching Directions. Place the central square of the pattern in the middle of the canvas and outline it with color #1. Work the square at upper right of canvas in color #1 also. Work the next smaller square with extensions in color #2, noting the direction of intersections.

Finally, work the color #3, as diagrammed, finishing one fourth of the pattern. Continue, completing one fourth of the pattern at a time. Recommended background stitch is diagonal tent. The finished pattern measures 8½" square when worked on #14 canvas.

Double Wedding Ring

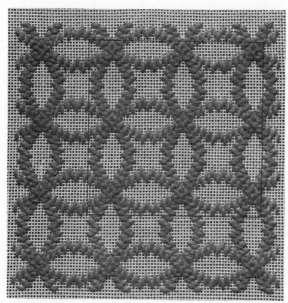

(See p. 75) Henry Ford Museum   Baltimore Museum of Art

The Double Wedding Ring pattern became popular after the Civil War. It was difficult to piece successfully because of its curves. As the name implies, the Double Wedding Ring pattern was often used as a bride's quilt, the most elaborate of the traditional thirteen quilts that brides were supposed to have in their hope chests on their wedding day. The bride's quilt was not even contemplated until the girl was engaged, and it was so elaborately pieced and quilted that it became a treasured showpiece. Perhaps that is why many bride's quilts still exist today—they were only used on special occasions.

Stitching Directions. This was a difficult quilt to piece and it is a difficult pattern to stitch. It is a challenge to the experienced needlewoman and is to be avoided by the beginner.

Begin in the center of the canvas with the diamond-shaped stitch. The needle always goes down in the center hole. Work the first circle. Then stitch an intersecting circle. At the intersections, allow the stitches to cross each other as diagrammed. Continue adding circles.

For the background, connect the sides of each ellipse by straight stitches. Begin filling the central diamonds by bringing your needle up in the middle hole. Work a straight stitch over 5 threads, sharing the hole with the Wedding Ring. Work 3 such stitches from the middle hole to each of the 3 remaining sides, forming a cross. Fill in each "V" so formed with smaller straight stitches following the direction of the central stitch. The intersections of the four quarters will form an "X." The finished pattern measures 7″ square when worked on #14 canvas.

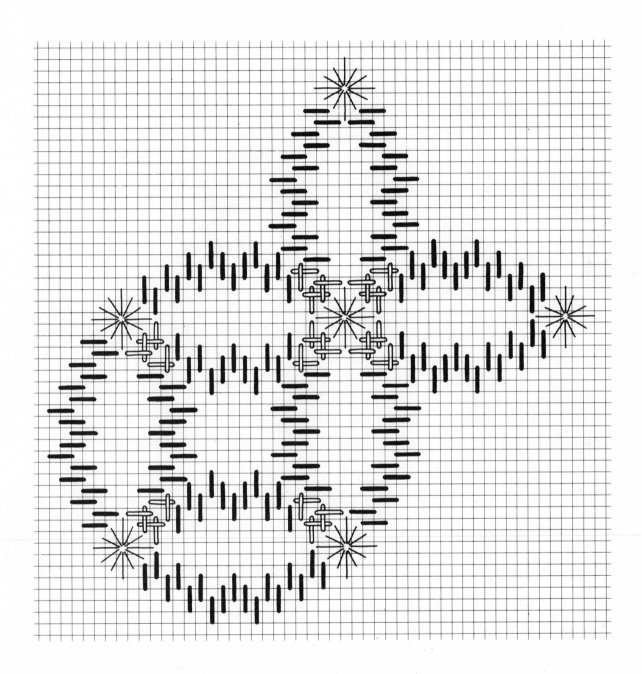

Log Cabin / Barn Raising

(See p. 72) Newark Museum Smithsonian Institution

The Log Cabin pattern is pieced from slender oblong patches of equal width but different lengths. The design is composed of inter-locking pieces much as the pioneer cabins were built of inter-locking "logs." In early colonial times, the quilts were made of woolen scraps. As life became easier, cottons and silks were used until, in Victorian times, the pattern was often worked with elegant silks and velvets.

Variations on the popular design soon developed—their differing effects depended upon the positioning of light and dark areas. This one is called Barn Raising.

All Log Cabin patterns are large designs composed of smaller modules. Only the use of color determines whether the final effect is softly antique or wildly contemporary.

Stitching Directions. Begin in the center of the canvas and stitch one block as diagrammed with all diagonal stitches running in the same direction. Work the remaining three center blocks so that the diagonals form a diamond. Stitch the outside blocks, working the dark shades first to correspond with the picture. For a square outline instead of an octagon, complete the corner squares with dark triangles. Do not pull the yarn tight, as all the stitches in one quadrant go in the same direction diagonally and the canvas can easily warp out of shape. Use a frame if you have one. The finished pattern measures 10¼" square when worked on #14 canvas.

Log Cabin / Light and Dark

(See p. 71)　State Historical Society of Iowa　Valentine Museum

This Log Cabin variation can be worked two ways—as pictured with a light center and dark frame, and the reverse—with a dark center and a light frame. Among such Log Cabin variations were the Straight Furrow, Courthouse Steps, Light and Dark, Barn Raising, Windmill Blades, Church Steps, and the most complex of all—the Pineapple.

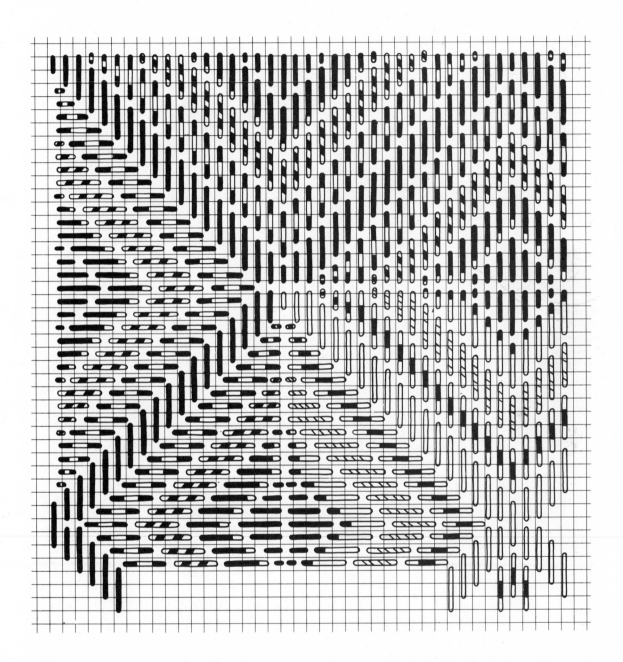

Stitching Directions. To cover a larger area, alternate a light frame with a dark frame. Start in the center of any block and stitch the "X." Complete the center and work the frame. The finished pattern measures 5½″ square when worked on #14 canvas.

Pineapple

(See p. 72)   Metropolitan Museum of Art   Victoria and Albert Museum

In eighteenth and nineteenth century America, the pineapple was a widely used symbol of hospitality, appearing in wood carvings, on furniture, in brass finials and on embroideries. Many varieties of intricate appliquéd Pineapple Quilts have come down to us from the early 1800s, but in the simpler patchwork, the favorite pineapple was this variation of the old Log Cabin pattern. The design's popularity reached its peak just before and after the Civil War, and was sometimes known as Windmill Blades.

The stitch used to create the diagonal pineapples is the Bayeux stitch, so called because it was used by William the Conqueror's wife, Queen Mathilda, and her ladies to work the Bayeux tapestry. This famous eleventh century embroidery, 230′ x 19½″, tells the story of the Norman invasion of England in 1066. Laid work, of which this stitch is an example, was a favorite of early New England embroiderers.

Stitching Directions. Center the pattern. Work the straight stitches in color #1 and diagonal stitches in color #2. Stitch all color #1 first. Fill in with progressively longer stitches to form pineapples in color #2. Keep your tension even and the yarn flattened. The longest of the pineapple stitches are much too long to wear well. Fasten them down by laying a trellis of long stitches in color #3 over the top according to the diagram. Attach the intersections of the trellis to the canvas by a small couching stitch in color #4 as diagrammed. The finished pattern measures 10½″ square when worked on #14 canvas.

Flowers, Leaves, and Trees

American Floral

Virginia Lily *(See p. 19)*
Denver Art Museum   Philadelphia Museum of Art

Day Lily *(See p. 19)*

Life in new America was down to earth. Elaborate flower designs, often called "tulips," that had been brought from England by the colonists, soon became simplified and naturalistic. The four quilt patterns shown here illustrate what happened to one English pattern after it emigrated.

The symbolic Lily of Purity in Elizabethan England was transplanted virtually intact to the colonies. It was called the Virginia Lily or North Carolina Lily, depending upon where the quilt was made.

Nature soon influenced Art in America. The Virginia Lily grew less

Ohio Peony *(See p.18)*
Newark Museum Henry Ford Museum

Kansas Sunflower *(See p.18)*

stylized and changed into the more natural Day Lily pattern.

As settlers moved West, the flowers around them changed and so did their quilt patterns. The Lilies of Virginia and North Carolina gained two new petals and a calyx in Ohio, and became the Ohio Peony.

Further West, the Peony added another two petals, and was transformed into the Kansas Sunflower. Thus the American colonists took a formalized symbol and gave it not one, but many new faces—all derived from the realities of the New World.

Stitching Directions. Work the flowers first. Then stitch the calyx of the flower and the triangular flowerpot. Work the background in diagonal tent stitch. The flower may be set within a diamond (see Backgrounds, p. 164) with Hungarian stitch around the diamond, or the entire background can be stitched in diagonal tent. Use chain stitch to make the stem on top of the background.

When stitching the Kansas Sunflower, work cross stitches in center as diagrammed.

These four flowers are very attractive worked on the same piece of canvas as a pillow. Use the long-armed cross stitch to divide the flowers and as a border (see Fans, p. 138). Each flower measures 3½″ square when worked on #14 canvas.

Virginia Lily Variation

(See p. 76)

The Virginia or North Carolina Lily variation is enlarged by increasing the length and number of stitches in each segment of the design and by using #10 instead of #14 canvas. Work it in the same sequence of steps as its smaller version on p. 108.

Stitching Directions. The top flower's petals are worked straight over 10 threads of the canvas. Its calyx is worked diagonally in two sections— each section covers 10 threads at longest point. The two sections share holes down the center of the triangle. The side flow-ers have petals stitched diagonally over 7 threads. Their calyxes are worked straight in two parts with the longest stitch over 11 threads. The flowerpot is worked in four sections diagonally. The longest stitch in each section covers 7 threads. The stems are done in the long armed cross and the background is the Hungarian stitch worked vertically within the diamond and horizontally outside it. The diamond itself is outlined in backstitch over two threads. The finished pattern measures 10″ square when worked on #10 canvas.

Tulip

(See p. 19)

The tulip was a flower that Northern European immigrants knew well. Stylized tulip motifs were frequently used in seventeenth century European art, and tulip patterns came to America in many guises. Quilt patterns now called Peony, Sunflower, and Lily all arrived in America under the title "tulip," only to have their names changed to conform to the wild flowers of this new land.

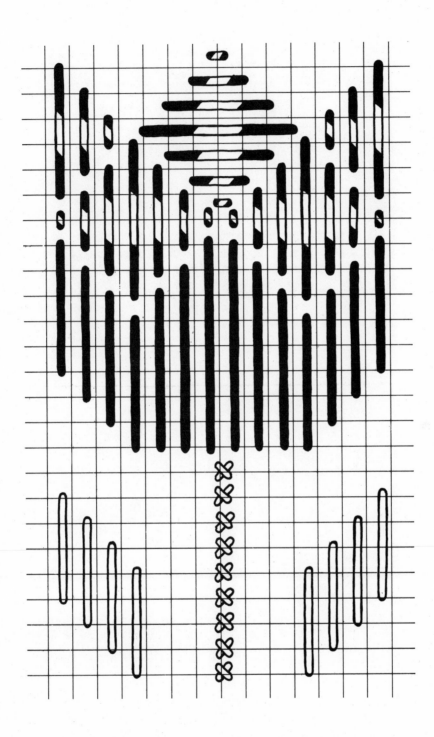

Stitching Directions. First work the tulip's top in color #1. Then stitch the flower's bottom in color #2, a darker shade of color #1. Work the stem and leaves in color #3 as diagrammed. This makes a good border or, when staggered, an overall pattern. The recommended background stitch is diagonal tent. Each flower measures 1½" x 2" when worked on #14 canvas.

Basket

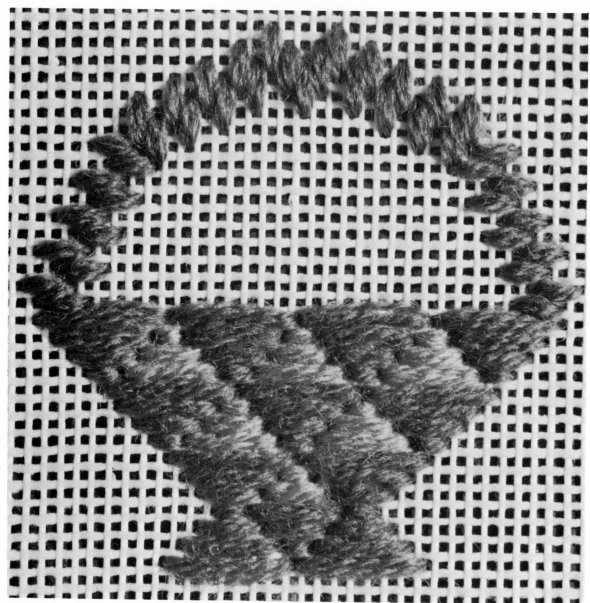

(See p.18)　Henry Ford Museum　Warren County Historical Society Museum

Baskets were favorite quilt patterns throughout the nineteenth century. Names such as Grandmother's Basket, Cherry Basket and Flower Basket were chosen to correspond with the basket's contents rather than the baskets themselves. These tended to follow the general pattern stitched here.

Baskets were filled with flowers, fruit or left empty to form an interesting pattern in themselves.

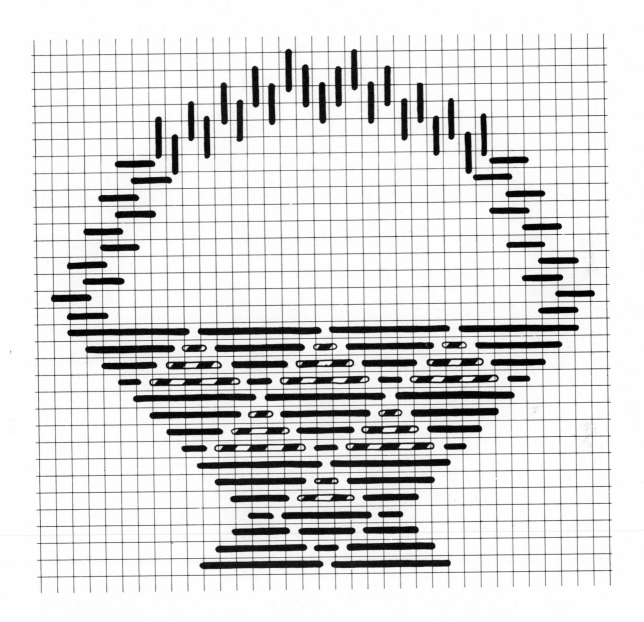

Stitching Directions. Work basket in color #1 and #2 as diagrammed. Stitch handle in color #1. For a flower basket, leave out basket's handle and instead, insert the Ohio Peony, the Kansas Sunflower, or the Virginia Lily. Center and position the bottoms of the lower two flowers on the rim of the basket and work the flowers from there. The recommended background stitch is diagonal tent. The finished pattern measures 2¾" x 2½" when worked on #14 canvas.

Forbidden Fruit Tree

(See p. 76)

In the Bible, the forbidden fruit tree was the cause of Adam and Eve's downfall and their subsequent expulsion from the Garden of Eden. The Bible and its stories were much on the minds of our forebears and form the subjects for many of the patterns in this book.

The Forbidden Fruit Tree is an explosive design with dramatic impact. Take note of the braided stitch climbing up the tree trunk—the snake?

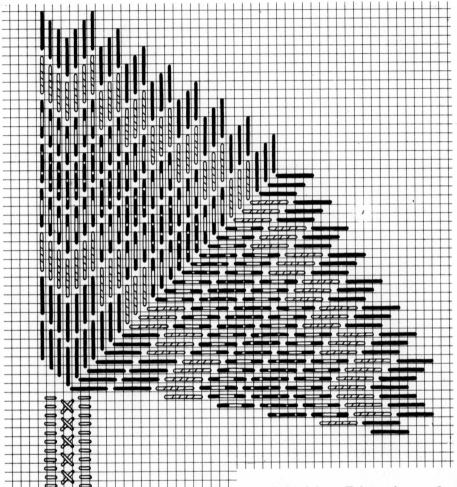

Stitching Directions. Start in the middle of the canvas and work the center stitches in your darkest shade of green, color #1. Work next the two rings in progressively lighter shades of green, #2 and #3. Stitch the following ring in a bright color, #4. Work the next three rings in colors #3, #2, and #1. Stitch the trunk with the long armed cross down the center and straight stitches on either side. The recommended background stitch is diagonal tent. For the border, (see Forbidden Fruit, p. 154). Including border, the finished pattern measures 10½″ square when worked on #14 canvas.

Tree of Life

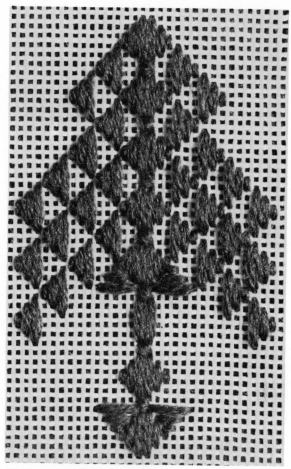

(See p. 19)   Henry Ford Museum

The Tree of Life motif originated in India. During the seventeenth century, textiles printed with this and other patterns were imported into Western Europe by the British East India Company and immediately won favor. Thus, many English women were familiar with the Tree of Life when they moved to America. Through the years, the print inspired crewel embroideries, samplers, and later, patchwork quilts. The quilt from which this design was derived was pieced about 1860.

Stitching Directions. Start at the top of the tree and work the trunk down to its base, following the diagram. Add cross stitches between the diamonds of the trunk. Work the leaves and base as diagrammed. Note that the diamonds of the trunk have two center stitches of equal length. Stitch the background by completing each diamond with the background color. Remaining background may be done in identical diamonds (see Tree of Life Variation, p. 122) stitched in the background color, or in diagonal tent stitch. The finished pattern measures 2¼″ x 3¾″ when worked on #14 canvas.

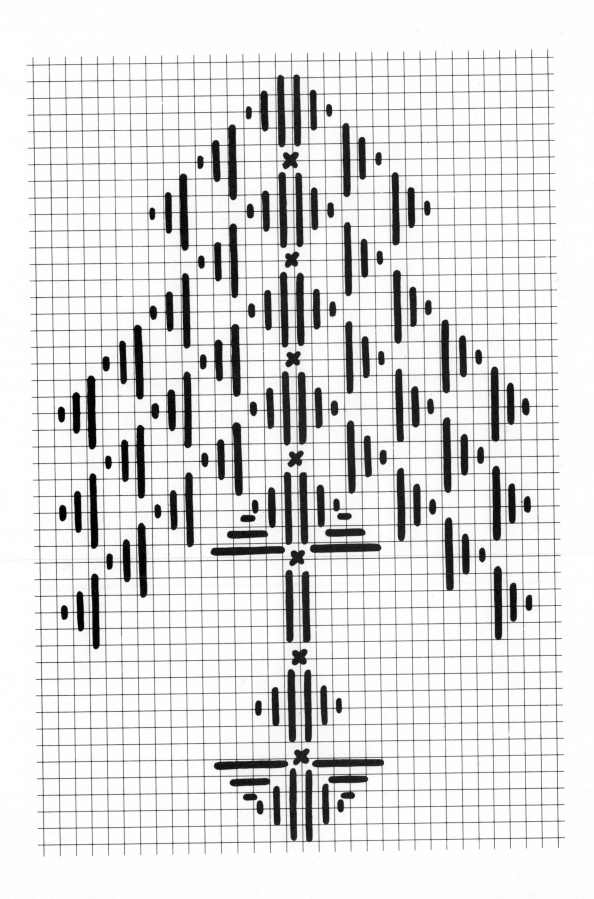

Tree of Life Variation

(See p. 19)

The Tree of Life variation is enlarged by increasing the length and number of stitches in each segment of the design and by using #10 instead of #14 canvas.

Stitching Directions. Center the tree in the middle of the canvas. In color #1 stitch the eight diamonds composing the trunk using horizontal straight stitches over 2, 4, 6, 8, 6, 4, 2 threads of canvas. Skip two threads (one hole) between each diamond. For the first leaf, work a vertical triangle, by connecting the side points of two diamonds with vertical straight stitches over 8, 6, 4, 2 threads. The top and bottom stitches of each leaf will share holes with the next. Position the leaves as shown in the picture, 14 to a side. Make two of the trunk diamonds into large triangles by adding a horizontal triangle (identical in thread count to the leaves) to each side of the diamonds. Connect the trunk diamonds with a cross stitch in color #2. Fill in the blank sections of the tree with background color #3 and complete the remaining background with diamonds identical to those composing the trunk.

The border is an enlarged version of the Wild Goose Chase border on p. 157 combined with the Gobelin border, p. 147. The Wild Goose Chase border is made up of diagonal blocks over 8 threads using color #1 for the triangles, color #2 for background, and color #3 for the longest stitch. The Gobelin border is worked over 5 threads using color #2 and over 2 threads in color #3. This Tree of Life variation, as photographed, is stitched in the shape of a brick cover. The finished Tree of Life pattern without the borders measures 3½″ x 6″ when worked on #10 canvas.

Little Beech Tree

(See p.18)   University of Kansas Museum of Art

Beech leaves are dark on top and lighter on their undersides. They appear two-toned when ruffled by the wind, an effect that has been captured with great charm in this old quilt pattern.

One variation of this design is called George Washington's Cherry Tree and is, basically, the Little Beech Tree with alternating green and red patches.

Stitching Directions. Center the top of the trunk at the middle of the canvas and stitch it following the diagram. Count up 22 threads from the

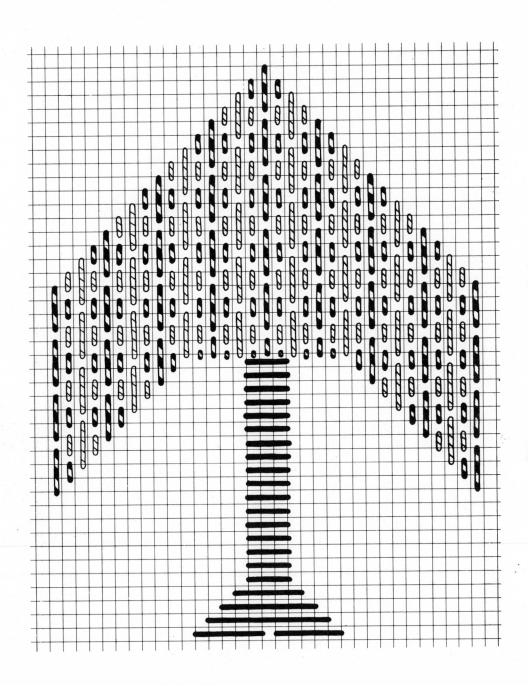

center of the trunk and stitch one Hungarian stitch in dark green. Work the second row in a lighter green. Working in horizontal rows, alternate your colors as shown in the diagram until the leaves are completed. Add a bright touch with a French knot in a gay color. The recommended background stitch is diagonal tent.

To stitch George Washington's Cherry Tree, use red instead of light green and eliminate the French knot. The finished pattern measures 2½″ x 3¼″ when worked on #14 canvas.

North American Leaves

English Ivy Leaf *(See p.18)*

In their new world of forests and deep woods, the settlers of America were always aware of trees. Timber was the main source of heat and shelter. Woodlands had to be cleared, with great effort, to make way for farmlands. And beyond the small settlements stretched the forests. So it is not surprising that trees and their leaves appear often on antique quilts. The four shown on these pages come from very different parts of the country, but all show a keen observation of nature and the simplification of natural forms into geometric patterns.

The Sweet Gum Leaf of the South and the Maple of the North can be combined with English Ivy Leaf and the abstract Autumn Leaf to form a four-part pillow. Use the long-armed cross stitch to divide the flowers and as a border (see Fans, p. 138).

The leaves may be set within a diamond (see Backgrounds, p. 164) with the Hungarian stitch around the diamond. Alternately, you could work the entire background in diagonal tent stitch. All leaves measure 3½″ square when worked on #14 canvas.

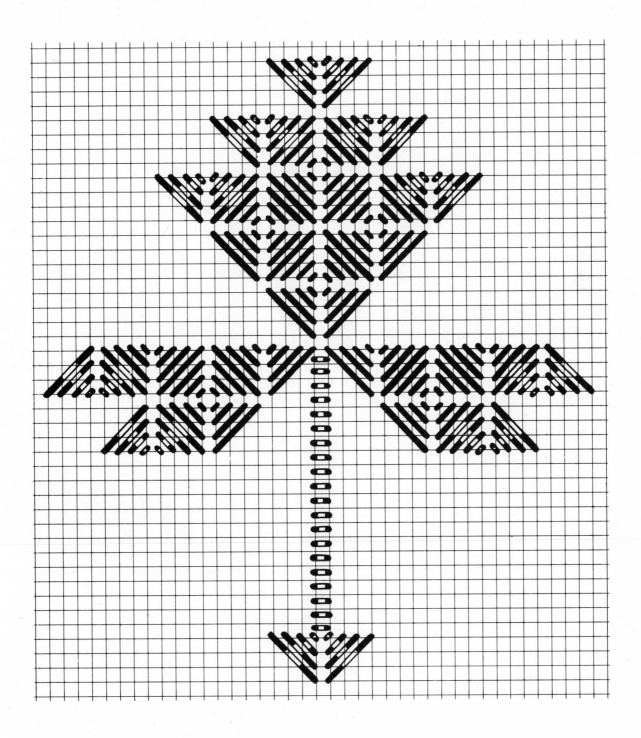

Stitching Directions for English Ivy Leaf. Center the middle of the leaf on the canvas. Work the top and side of the leaf in dark green. Stitch leaf tips in lighter green. Work the stem and base in the lighter green also.

Maple Leaf *(See p.18)*

Stitching Directions for Maple Leaf. This leaf may be stitched using either one or two colors. To work it in one color, follow the black and white photograph, alternating the slant of the squares. To work the leaf in two colors, follow the color photograph on p. 18. First stitch the triangular portion of the leaf in color #1. Then work the leaf tips and stem in color #2. Finally, work the base in color #1.

Sweet Gum Leaf *(See p.18)*

Stitching Directions for Sweet Gum Leaf. Place the bottom of "V" at the center of your canvas and stitch the top of the leaf. Stitch both sides of leaf. Stitch the stem and base, allowing your diagonal stitches to overlap the straight stitches where stem and leaf join.

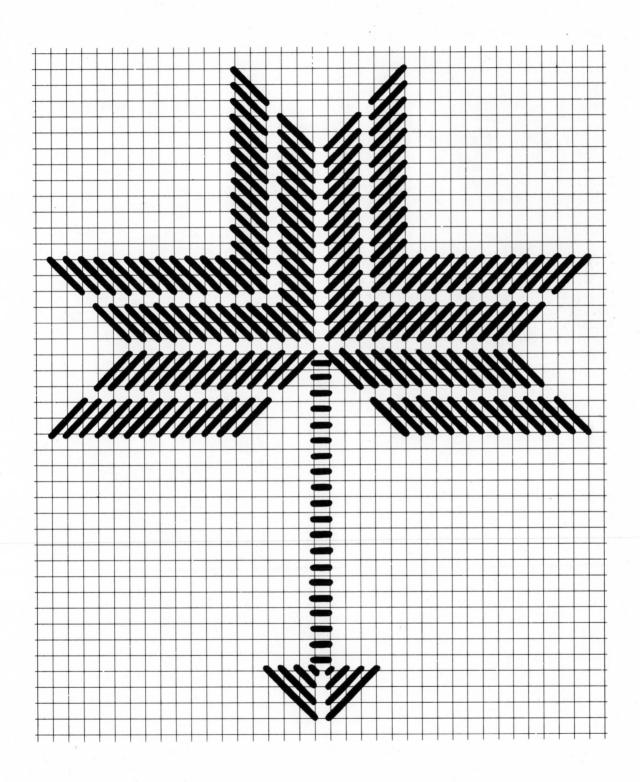

Autumn Leaf *(See p.18)*

Stitching Directions for Autumn Leaf. Work the four central squares in color #1, so that their longest stitches meet in the same hole. Stitch the rectangles that enclose the central squares in color #2. Work outer squares and triangles in color #1, following the diagram. Finally, work the stem and base in color #2, allowing the diagonal stitches to overlap straight stitches where the stem and leaf join.

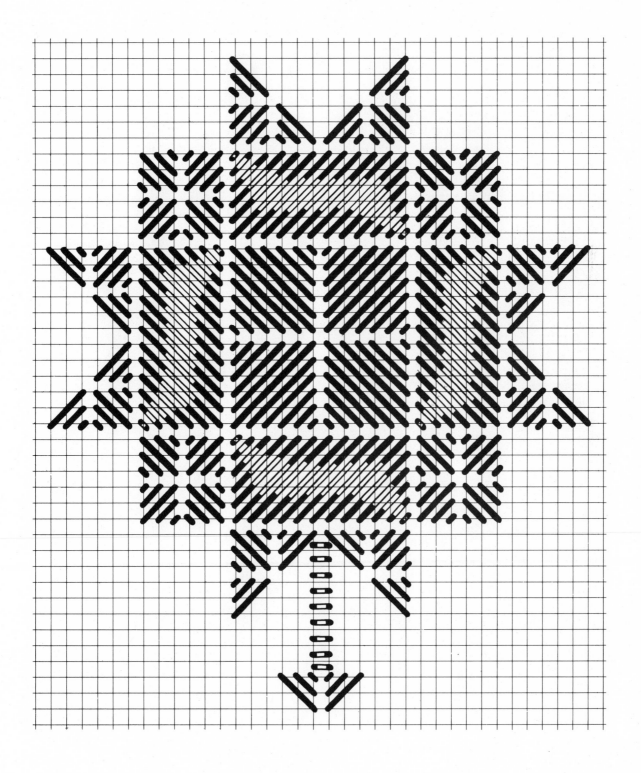

Samplers

Jack in the Box

(See p. 76)

Simple quilt patterns, when enlarged, make marvelous outlines for needlepoint samplers. Many of the geometric designs in this book may be used in this fashion.

The following stitches were used to work this sampler: diamond eye, oriental, double straight cross, byzantine, Hungarian, diagonal, straight Milanese, diagonal Milanese, upright Gobelin, long armed cross, bargello.

The finished pattern measures 9″ square when worked on #14 canvas.

Octagons

(See p. 76)   Henry Ford Museum

This nameless octagonal design is, as far as we can determine, a one-of-a-kind pattern.

The design is a sophisticated one that creates a controlled optical illusion. We have used it as the basis for a needlepoint sampler. For the beginner, enjoy another pattern and save this one for later!

The following stitches were used to work this sampler: leaf, Smyrna cross, mosaic, diamond eye, diagonal, byzantine, Hungarian, flat, double straight cross, rice, continuous mosaic. Fill in the remaining octagons with other stitches.

The finished pattern measures 11½″ square when worked on #14 canvas.

Fans

(See p. 73) Arizona Historical Society   Henry Ford Museum

After the Civil War, no lady of fashion would have felt properly gowned without her fan. Not unexpectedly, fan patterns became popular quilt designs in the 1870s. They were often worked in silks and velvets on what we now call crazy quilts, but what were then known as parlor throws—luxurious quilts kept in the parlor and used as coverings for after-dinner naps. Parlor throws are easy to recognize because of their dimensions. They are too small to fit even a single bed.

Stitching Directions. The fan pillow shown is a sampler. It's easy to design fans when you realize that an eight-pointed star without its points is a circle. Divide the circle in quarters and you have four fans. Any eight-pointed star pattern in this book can be used for a fan. In this sampler, the fan at left center is the Blue Star (p. 26), the one at top center is a Star of Bethlehem (p. 30). The recommended background stitch is diagonal tent. Dividing strips and border are worked in long armed cross stitch. The finished pattern measures 11″ square when worked on #14 canvas.

Borders and Backround Stitches

Gobelin Borders

(See p. 20)

Patterns were framed by borders, enclosed within lattices or stood alone, depending on the quilter's wishes. Latticework could outline or emphasize a design and borders could enlarge or frame. They serve the same functions in needlepoint as they did in quilting.

Stitching Directions. Large borders which need a certain number of threads to complete each segment should be planned completely before the project is begun. Smaller borders may be added after a central design is finished.

The Gobelin and Nine-Patch borders are infinitely expandable and can be made to fit any project. They are good choices if you want to add a border to a finished pattern.

The Sawtooth and Wild Goose Chase borders must reverse direction in the center of each side so that the corners can turn. Stitch as diagrammed.

1. Framed Sqaures
2. Double Gobelin
3. Nine Patch
4. Gobelin Lattice
5. Twisted Trail

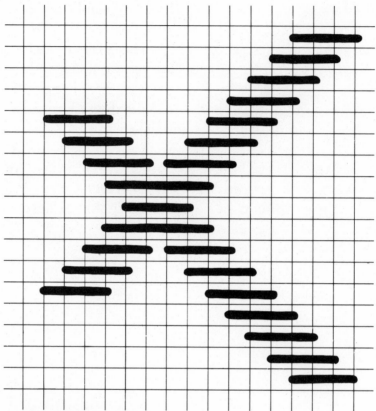

Gobelin Lattice

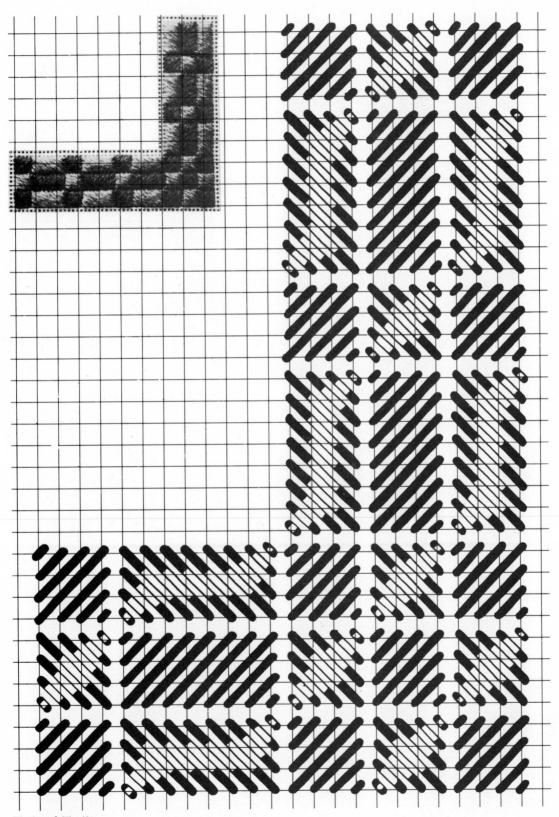

Twisted Trails

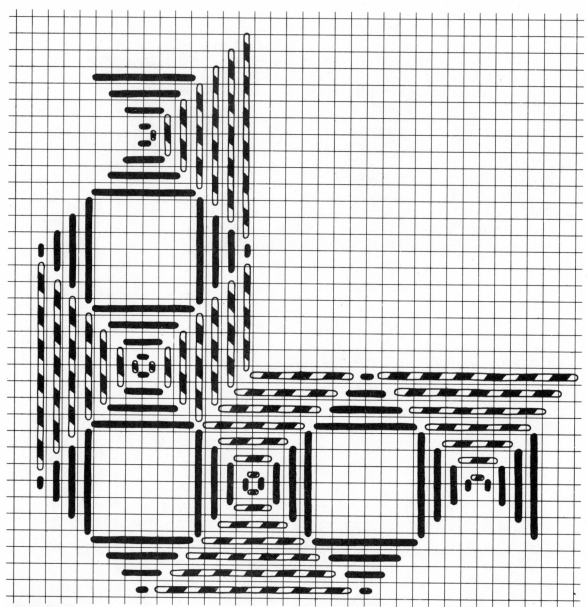

Framed Squares

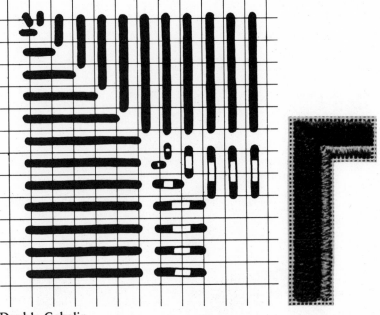

Double Gobelin

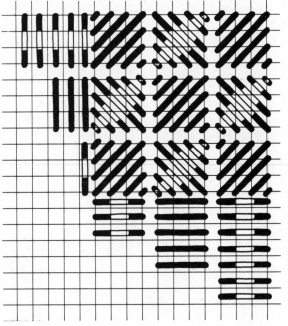

Nine Patch
Henry Ford Museum Smithsonian Institution

Star Borders

(See p. 20)

Lone Star *Newark Museum*

1. Lone Star
2. Star of LeMone
3. Seven Sisters

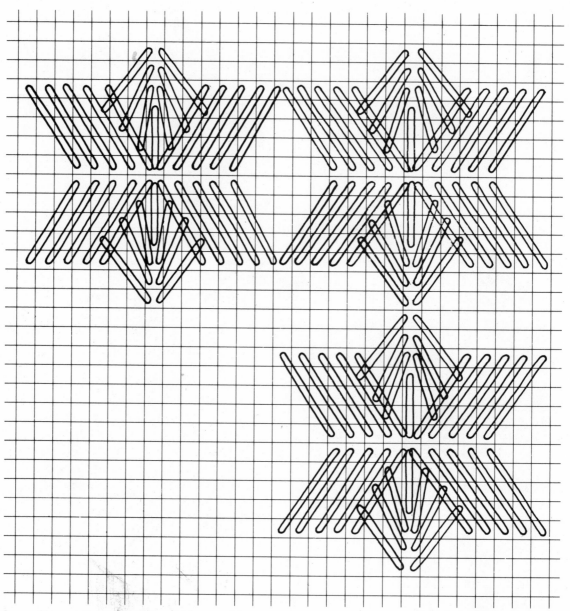

Seven Sisters *University of Kansas Museum of Art*

Star of LeMoyne *Smithsonian Institution*

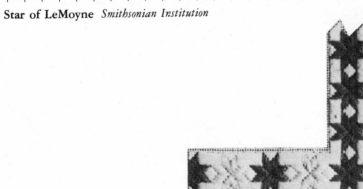

Ribbon Borders

(See p. 20)

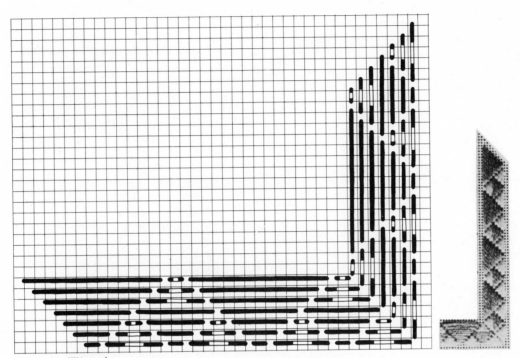

Triangle *Winterthur*

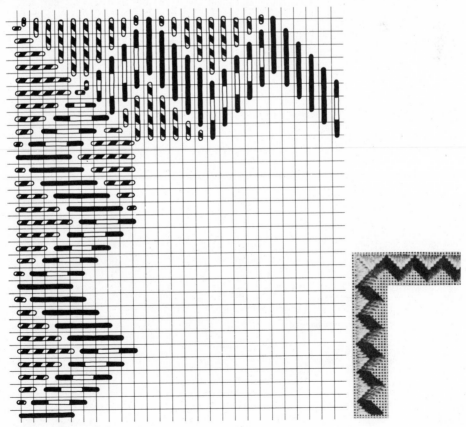

1. Twist and Turn
2. Ribbon
3. Wedding Ring
4. Forbidden Fruit
5. Triangle

Ribbon *Winterthur*

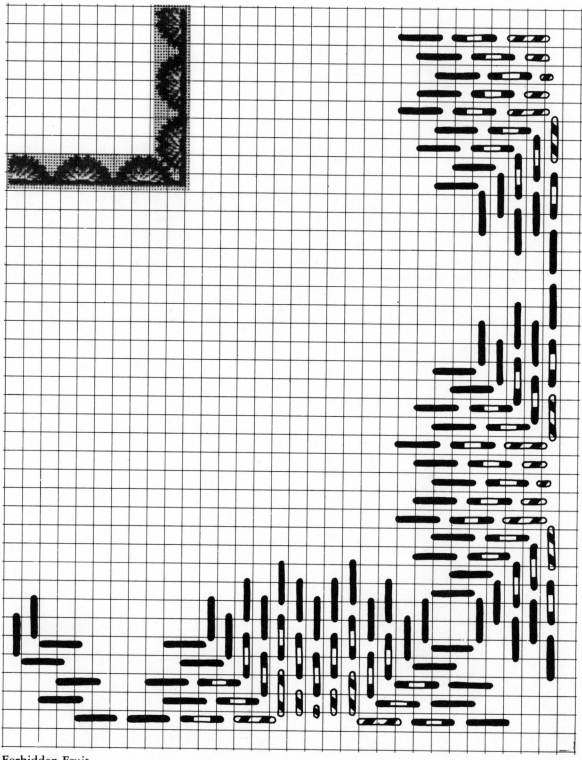

Forbidden Fruit

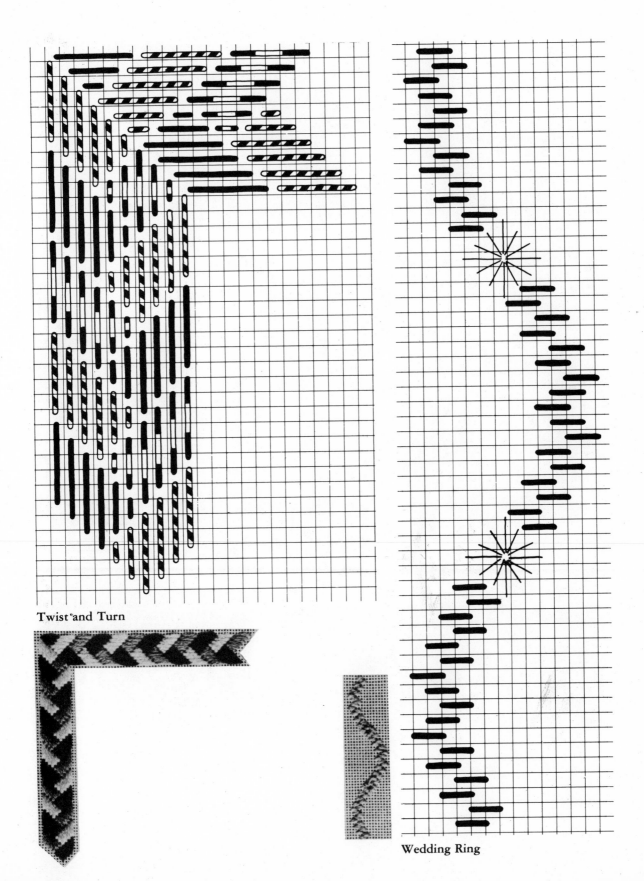

Twist and Turn

Wedding Ring

Wild Geese Borders

(See p. 20)

1. **Wild Goose Chase**
2. **Pinwheel**
3. **Wild Goose Chase Lattice**
4. **Sawtooth**

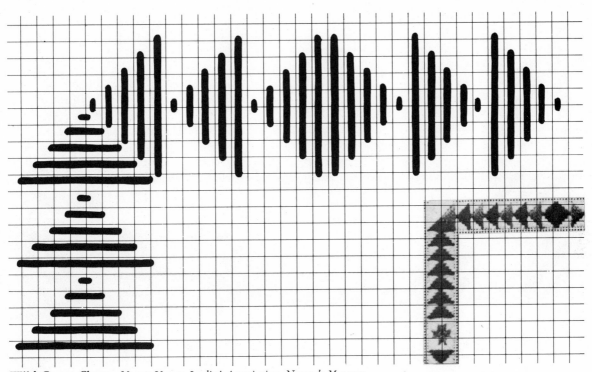

Wild Goose Chase *Mount Vernon Ladies' Association Newark Museum*

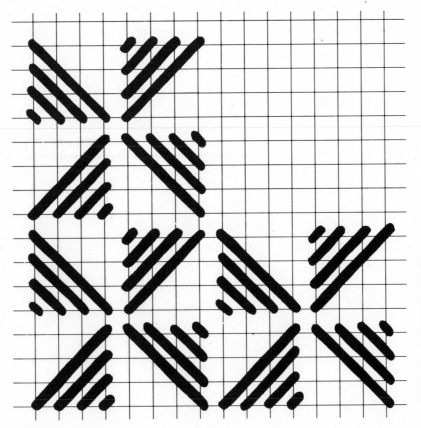

Pinwheel *Mount Vernon Ladies' Association*

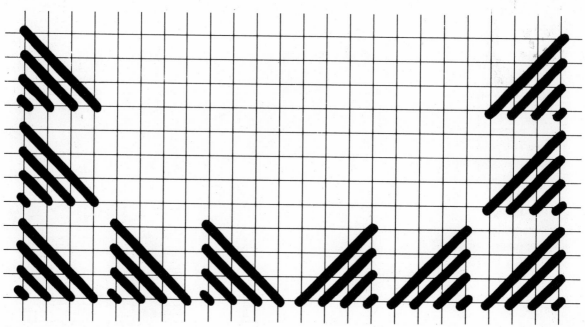

Sawtooth *Newark Museum*

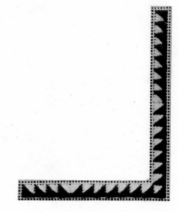

Wild Goose Chase Lattice *Smithsonian Institution*

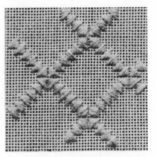

Splint Quilting

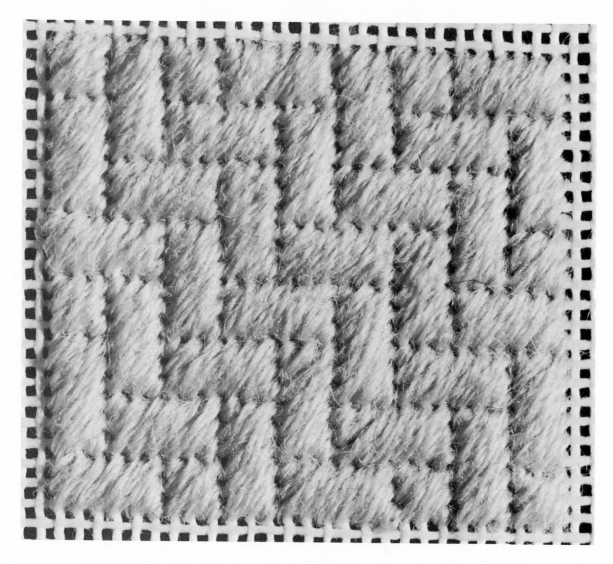

This textured stitch is derived from a quilting pattern in vogue in the eighteenth century. Just as the patchwork pattern is complemented by the quilting used to attach the filling and backing, so needlepoint designs can be made more beautiful by the choice of a harmonious background stitch. This stitch can be used as a background in one color, or it can be worked as a pattern in its own right, with varying colors.

The splint pattern was used in other crafts than quilting. Thin strips of wood or "splints" were woven into chair seats and bricks were laid into paths according to this pattern. In general it was an orderly way to arrange materials in a design.

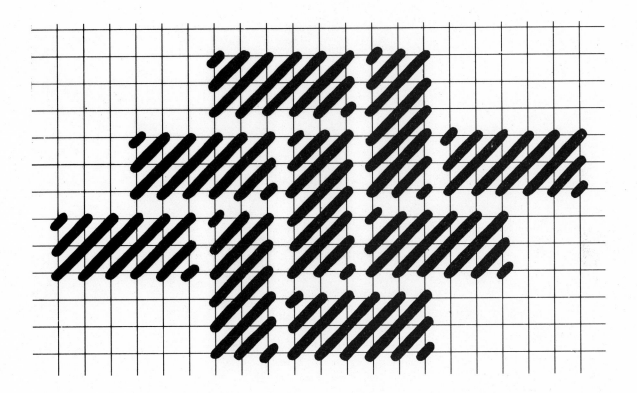

Hungarian Stitch

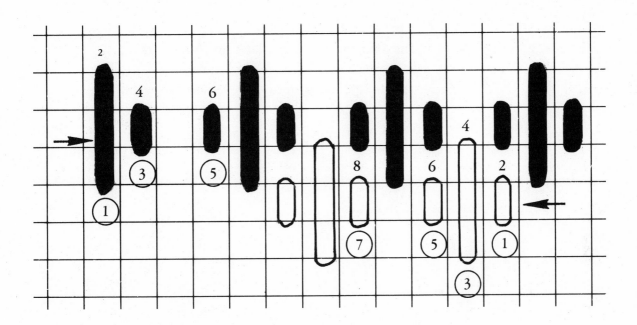

To enclose a flower or leaf pattern within a frame of Hungarian stitch, center the design within a square of 48 threads per side. Work a straight stitch over 4 threads in the upper left corner as diagrammed. Next to it, work a stitch over 2 threads, centered on the first stitch. Skip two threads and work a row of five Hungarian stitches (see photograph). Begin the next row as pictured. The right edge of the stitching forms a slanted line. Continue to work, keeping the left margin straight. Decrease the right margin by one Hungarian stitch per row until one quarter of the background is completed. Work the remaining three quarters in the same way with all Hungarian stitches in the same direction. Work small straight compensating stitches along the top and bottom edges (see photograph).

The work pictured measures 3½″ square when worked on #14 canvas and covers 48 threads in each direction.

Background Stitches

Many of the designs in this book are stitched on bare canvas for the sake of clarity. The diagonal tent or basketweave (see diagram #1) is the best known background stitch, and is specified with certain patterns. Directions for other background stitches can be found in basic needlepoint books.

The flower and leaf patterns in this book lend themselves to enclosure within a diamond formed by the Hungarian stitch (see preceding page).

The long armed cross (diagram #2) can divide areas of background (see Fans, p. 138) or provide a finishing touch to edges. The chain stitch (diagram #3) forms the stems of flowers and should be worked on top of the diagonal tent background.

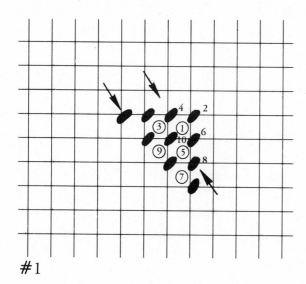

#1

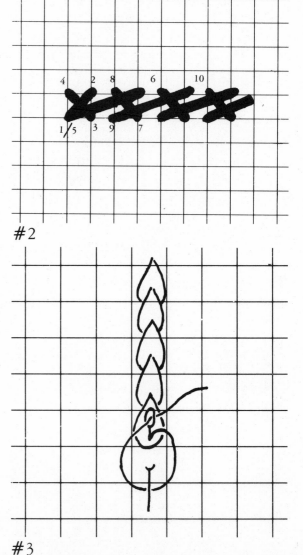

#2

#3

Canvas-Needle-Yarn Chart

The designs in this book specify the gauge canvas to use, the gauge indicates the type of wool, the wool determines the number of strands of yarn per needleful.

This chart is based on the amount of yarn necessary for a diagonal stitch. When working with a straight stitch, one more strand of yarn may be needed to cover the canvas well. Individual yarns vary slightly in thickness, and it would be wise to stitch a small area on the margin with the amount of yarn specified. Should the canvas not be adequately covered, add another strand of wool, if using stranded yarn. If your yarn is not stranded, paint the area of canvas with waterproof magic markers or acrylic artist's paints in yarn color. Allow the area to dry before stitching and any canvas that shows through will not be apparent.

GAUGE CANVAS	YARN TYPE	AVERAGE NUMBER OF STRANDS NEEDED PER NEEDLEFUL
5	Rug	1 strand
	Tapestry	2 strands
	Persian	8 strands
7	Rug	1 strand
	Persian	4 single strands
10	Tapestry	1 strand
	Persian	3 single strands
	Crewel	5 strands
12	Persian	2 single strands
	Crewel	4 strands
14	Persian	2 single strands
	Crewel	3 single strands
16/18	Persian	1 single strand
	Crewel	2 strands

The correct size needle is one which will easily hold the amount of yarn necessary, without distorting the canvas meshes as the needle eye passes through.

Canvas Conversion Chart

Use this chart to determine the amount of canvas needed for a design when you change the gauge of the canvas.

Example: On #14 canvas, a design measures 11″. If it is worked on #10 canvas, it would measure 11″ x 1.4″ or slightly over 15″. A minimum of 1½″ of unworked canvas should extend beyond the work on all four sides for blocking and finishing.

Row A is the known gauge of canvas. Row B is desired gauge. Multiply the number in the square where Row A and Row B intersect, times the known dimension of the finished design, to find the area that would be covered.

A. KNOWN GAUGE	B. DESIRED GAUGE					
	5	10	12	14	16	18
5	1	.5	.4	.35	.3	.27
10	2	1	.8	.7	.6	.5
12	2.4	1.2	1	.9	.8	.7
14	2.8	1.4	1.2	1	.9	.8
16	3.2	1.6	1.3	1.1	1	.9
18	3.6	1.8	1.5	1.3	1.1	1

Museums

Many of the patterns which inspired the canvas work embroidery designs in this book can be seen on quilts in museum collections throughout the United States. When we know that an example of a particular quilt design is in a museum or historical society, the institution's name is given. Patterns which are not so designated have been derived from privately owned quilts.

The following is a list of museums which own outstanding quilts. While it does not pretend to be complete, it does form a starting point for the reader who wants to learn more.

Museum exhibits change, and all quilts are not on display at all times. It may be necessary to make a special arrangement to see the quilt in which you are interested, so call or write before you visit the museum.

Arizona Historical Society, Tucson, Arizona

Baltimore Museum of Art, Baltimore, Maryland

Connecticut Historical Society, Hartford, Connecticut

Denver Art Museum, Denver, Colorado

Henry Ford Museum, Dearborn, Michigan

Henry Francis duPont Winterthur Museum, Winterthur, Delaware

Metropolitan Museum of Art, American Wing, New York City

Mount Vernon Ladies' Association, Mount Vernon, Virginia

Newark Museum, Newark, New Jersey

Philadelphia Museum of Art, Philadelphia, Pennsylvania

Shelburne Museum, Shelburne, Vermont

Smithsonian Institution, Washington, D.C.

Society for the Preservation of New England Antiquities, Boston, Massachusetts

Spring Mill State Park, Mitchell, Indiana

State Historical Society of Iowa, Iowa City, Iowa

Old Sturbridge Village, Sturbridge, Massachusetts

University of Kansas Museum of Art, Lawrence, Kansas

Valentine Museum, Richmond, Virginia

Victoria and Albert Museum, London, England

Warren County Historical Society Museum, Lebanon, Ohio

Bibliography

Ambuter, Carolyn. *Complete Book of Needlepoint*. New York: Thomas Y. Crowell and Workman Publishing Co., Inc., 1972.

Brightbill, Dorothy. *Quilting As a Hobby*. New York: Sterling Publishing Co., Inc., 1963.

Carlisle, Lilian Baker. *Pieced Work and Applique Quilts at Shelburne Museum*. Shelburne, Vt.: The Shelburne Museum, 1957.

Caulfield, S. F. A. *Encyclopedia of Victorian Needlework*. 1887. Reprinted New York: Dover Publications Inc., 1972.

Colby, Averil. *Samplers*. Newton Centre, Mass.: Charles T. Branford Co., 1965.

Fennelly, Catherine. *Textiles in New England, 1790-1840*. Sturbridge, Mass.: Old Sturbridge Village, 1961.

Finley, Ruth E. *Old Patchwork Quilts and the Women Who Made Them*. 1929. Reprint. Newton Centre, Mass.: Charles T. Branford Co., 1970.

Hall, Carrie A., and Kretsinger, Rose G. *The Romance of the Patchwork Quilt in America*. 1935. Reprint. New York: Bonanza Books.

Hinson, Dolores A. *Quilting Manual*. New York: Hearthside Press, Inc., 1966.

Hinson, Dolores A. *A Quilter's Companion*. New York: Arco Publishing Co., Inc., 1973.

Holstein, Jonathan. *American Pieced Quilts*. Washington, D.C.: The Smithsonian Institution Traveling Exhibition Service, 1972.

Holstein, Jonathan. *The Pieced Quilt—An American Design Tradition*. New York: New York Graphic Society, 1973.

Ickis, Marguerite. *The Standard Book of Quilt Making and Collecting*. 1949. Reprint. New York: Dover Publications, Inc., 1959.

Ireys, Katharine. *The Encyclopedia of Canvas Embroidery Stitch Patterns*. New York: Thomas Y. Crowell Company, 1972.

Katzenberg, Dena S. *The Great American Cover-Up: Counterpanes of the Eighteenth and Nineteenth Centuries*. Baltimore, Md.: The Baltimore Museum of Art, 1971.

McKim, Ruby Short. *One Hundred and One Patchwork Patterns*. 1931. Reprint. New York: Dover Publications, Inc., 1962.

Robertson, Elizabeth Wells. *American Quilts*. New York: The Studio Publications, Inc., 1948.

Rosson, Lea. "Quilts at the University of Kansas Museum of Art." *Antiques*, December, 1973.

Safford, Carleton L., and Bishop, Robert. *America's Quilts and Coverlets*. New York: E. P. Dutton & Co., Inc., 1972.

Webster, Marie D. *Quilts: Their Story and How to Make Them*. 1915. Reprint. Detroit Mich.: Gale Research Co., 1973.

White, Margaret. *Quilts and Counterpanes in the Newark Museum*. Newark, N.J.: The Newark Museum, 1948.